KERALA

THE LAND OF PALMS

KERALA

THE LAND OF PALMS

I. H. HACKER

Followed by

BASIL MATHEWS, M. A.

GYAN

Published by

Gyan Publishing House
5, Ansari Road
Daryaganj, New Delhi-110002
Phone: 011-47034999, 9811692060
E-mail: books@gyanbooks.com

Distribution Network
gyanbooks.com
India, USA, Canada, UK, Australia, France

ISBN: 978-81-212-8658-9 (PB)
First Published, 1912

2nd Impression 2023

Printed at: Gyan Press, Delhi.

KERALA THE LAND OF PALMS
Author: I. H. Hacker

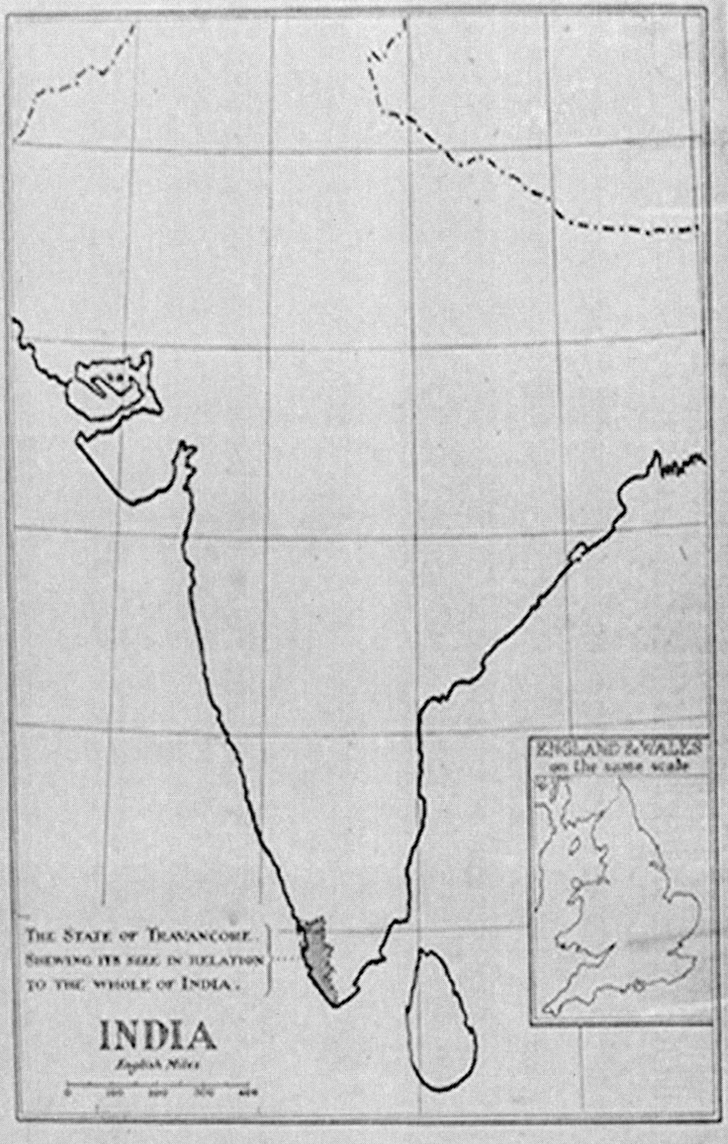
ENGLAND & WALES
on the same scale
THE STATE OF TRAVANCORE.
SHEWING ITS SIZE IN RELATION
TO THE WHOLE OF INDIA.
INDIA
English Miles

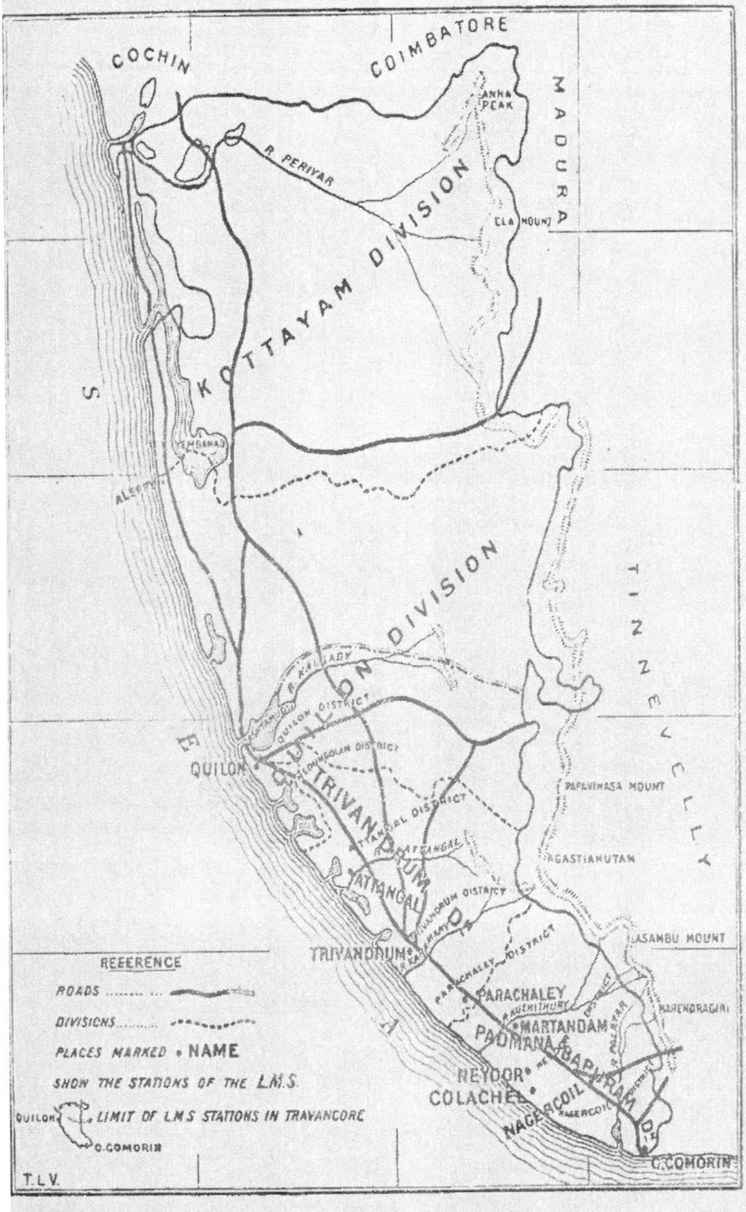
COCHIN
COIMBATORE
MADURA
ANNA PEAK
R. PERIYAR
KOTTAYAM DIVISION
QUILON DIVISION
TINNEVELLY
QUILON
QUILON DISTRICT
TRIVANDRUM
TRIVANDRUM D.
ATTANGAL
PAPAVINASA MOUNT
AGASTIANUTAM
ASAMBU MOUNT
MAHENDRAGIRI
PARACHALEY
PARACHALEY DISTRICT
MARTANDAM
PADMANABHAPURAM
NAGERCOIL
REYOOR
COLACHEL
C. COMORIN
REFERENCE
ROADS ....
DIVISIONS........
PLACES MARKED • NAME
SHOW THE STATIONS OF THE L.M.S.
LIMIT OF L.M.S STATIONS IN TRAVANCORE
QUILON
C. COMORIN
T.L.V.

KERALA
THE LAND OF PALMS

KERALA

THE LAND OF PALMS

By

I. H. HACKER

WITH FOUR COLOURED PLATES AND

SIXTY-THREE ILLUSTRATIONS

Followed by

THROUGH THE EYES OF THE ISLAND CHILDREN

By BASIL MATHEWS, M.A

London

LONDON MISSIONARY SOCIETY

16, NEW BRIDGE STREET, E.C

—

1912

BUTLER & TANNER,
THE SELWOOD PRINTING WORKS,
FROME, AND LONDON.

CONTENTS

LIST OF ILLUSTRATIONS IN COLOUR

LIST OF PLATES

LIST OF ILLUSTRATIONS IN THE TEXT

KERALA, THE LAND OF PALMS

CHAPTER I

THE LAND AND THE PEOPLE

WHERE is this country of Kerala? What kind of land is it? and what sort of people are they who live there and call it their home? It is a land of wandering beggars, pilgrims, strolling players, conjurors, snake-charmers, where people bathe the baby at the roadside and cut their hair in the street; where the sun is very hot and the hills are very high—a country of palm trees and streams, temples and crowded streets, tigers, bisons and elephants. It is the country that sends us pepper and coffee and tea.

I ask you to come with me. We will travel together along the roads, see how the people live, climb their hills, and talk of adventures. We will see the children at their play and in their schools, and we will see how in this beautiful land, amongst a simple and lovable people, the Gospel of our Lord and Saviour Jesus Christ is bringing blessing amongst them all.

If you take a map of India (look inside the cover) and mark down the most extreme southern point in that great country you will see that it is called Cape Comorin. Suppose we could take a boat at this point and sail northwards, along the west coast, we should see a low-lying well-wooded country, with a background of high mountains.

"THEY CUT THEIR HAIR IN THE STREET."

If we continued our voyage along this coast for about 150 miles, after passing such places as Trivandrum and Quilon (see page 11), we should reach a port called Alleppy. Leaving our vessel, we must travel by land eastwards for about fifty miles, when our progress would be stopped by a great chain of mountains running from north to south, for hundreds of miles through India, some of them six or seven thousand feet above the level of the sea. Climbing these mountains, we must then travel southwards for about 170 miles, until we descend at the most southern point of India and find ourselves at the place we started from, called Cape Comorin. We have rapidly run round a tract of country about the size of Wales, which contains three

ON THE BACKWATER, QUILON, TRAVANCORE.

million people. It is one of the fairest portions of India, and the people who live there are proud of their land.

We know how proud the people who live in Wales are of their lofty mountains and their lovely vales. In the same way the people who live in the land we are describing say, "Fair is the great land of India, but fairer than all is our beautiful Kerala, the land of Travancore."

There—at last I have mentioned one of the names of the country. Travancore = Tiru vitham codu, the abode of prosperity, is the name by which it is generally known. It is also called Malayalam; spell it backwards, spell it forwards, it is the same, and this word means hill and dale. Another name is Venad, the land of the shining ones, for the country is thought to be sacred. Kerala, a very sweet-sounding word, means a land of cocoa-nut palms, hence the title of this book. Another name is Tiru = holy, adi = foot, Desam = land (or the land which has the impress of the divine foot).

Here is the legend of how the battle-axe wielder (Parusa = axe, Rama = warrior) obtained this lovely land from the sea.

In ancient times the warriors, the men of blood, were doing deeds of shame and were over-running the earth. Religious places were destroyed, worshippers of the gods despised, and lawlessness covered the land. The pious men were represented by the Brahmins; the evil workers by the Kshatriya, or warrior race.

The Brahmins prayed to the gods, who sent Parasu Rama, as an incarnation of Vishnu, to right the wrong, punish the wicked and preserve the good (his image is on the cover). Armed with a battle-axe against which none could stand,

Parasu Rama attacked the warrior race, defeated the kings of this race in twenty-one great battles and restored order and peace to the country.

Parasu Rama retired to some mountains in the south of India to cleanse himself from the sin of the bloodshed he had caused. He won the favour of Varuna, the god of the seas.

Varuna said: "From the place you stand, throw your axe as far as you can into the sea, and from here to the place it falls the sea shall recede, and the land shall be yours." Parasu Rama whirled the axe three times round his head and gave it a mighty throw. The axe fell at the spot now called Cape Comorin, and the sea receded more than two hundred miles, leaving the land of Travancore dry land. Into this newly reclaimed land Parasu Rama brought Brahmins from all parts of India.

* * * * *

In Travancore the people have been less disposed to welcome anything new than in almost any other part of India, though the present Maharajah is more open-minded. The caste system is very rigidly kept. My readers will have heard of caste, but they will not be able really to understand it, because we have nothing like it in England. We have the classes: the King, the Clergy, the Army and Navy, the learned professions, the merchants, the skilled workers, the agricultural labourers. Caste recognizes these differences of class, but has made these classes into barriers which prevent people from ever passing from one class into another. Each caste is supposed to be as distinct from others as are the various species of animals, such as the horse, the ox, or the ass.

Here is the ancient story. The Supreme Spirit, wishing to create a being who should worship him and conduct worship for others, caused the Brahmins to spring from his head; the Brahmin therefore is a god upon earth. To keep order in the world the Supreme Spirit produced from his shoulders the Kshatriya, the fighting man. Then there was need for the merchant and skilled workmen. This third caste, the Vaishia, came from the thighs of the Divine being. Finally there was needed the man to till the soil and do the hard and servile work, so the Sudra came from the Divine feet. The great number of people who did not come under these four heads (out-castes) were considered as equal only to the lower animals and were treated as the off-scouring of the world.

These out-castes, who are the most numerous in Travancore, are much despised. They cannot use the same wells, they cannot touch the same cooking vessels, or visit the houses of the higher castes, and until lately they could not walk along the same roads. About two years ago, a poor hard-working man, connected with one of our churches, had been carrying a heavy load on his head for miles; almost fainting with the heat of the sun, he put down his burden and sat resting on the side of a public road. A few minutes afterwards, a proud high caste man came down the same public road. He carried an umbrella to shield himself from the rays of the sun, and he was attended by two servants. He passed this poor tired man, and because he did not get up and run away into a field sixty yards off, so that the high caste man should not be polluted, but simply lifted his hands in homage and said, "Salaam Eiyah," "Peace to you, sir," the caste man said, "Go thrash that man," and the servants did his bidding so thoroughly that the poor man was ill for days. This caste man, however, had forgotten that His Highness the Maharajah has issued a law which declared public roads were free for every class, caste or creed, and we were able under this law to get the proud man punished.

Travancore is one of the native states of India. That means that the country is not directly ruled by the British Government, but is ruled by a Hindu king called the Maharajah, in friendly alliance with the British Government. The present Maharajah is named Rama Vurma, K.G.C.S.I., and is one of the most enlightened chiefs of

India. He is very kindly disposed towards all movements which advance his country and people. At his capital he has magnificent public buildings, a large college for boys and girls, hospitals for the sick, and homes for lepers, beautiful public libraries and parks for his people, and he is honoured by high and low.

CHAPTER II

BY BULLOCK-CART AND BOAT

NOW let us start on our travels. Instead of beginning at Cape Comorin, and entering Travancore from the sea, we will go a little way along the east coast to a port called Tuticorin. After about two hours' ride in a train, we find ourselves at a place called Tinnevelli. Here we take bullock-cart.

You will see in the picture a rough cart, the body built of heavy wood, the wheels huge and unwieldy, no springs, covered by bent bamboo, over which are spread mats, and open at each end. It is drawn by two bullocks yoked together, and when we have good strong bullocks we can rush along at two and a half miles an hour! To make it comfortable, we get as much straw as possible, over it put a mat, and after telling the driver to start, lie down. Suppose we leave Tinnevelli at four in the afternoon, we reach the frontier of Travancore, a pass called Arumbulli in a gap between two mountains, at about eight next morning. We find ourselves in a broad road, well made, which takes us to Trevandrum, the capital.

On either side of the road have been planted large banyan trees, and as we travel onward, the

A Curious Way of Raising Water.

mountains on either side, the large forests of tall palmyra trees, the vast expanse of green rice fields, the passing of immense numbers of people, going to and from the different markets, in the distance the lofty towers of some temples, the bright sun lighting all with a golden glory, form a charming picture.

This picture shows a curious way of raising water, which has been in use for hundreds of years. A tall trunk of a palmyra tree is placed upright in the ground, rising to a height of about fifty feet; across this are fixed horizontal pieces of wood, heavier at one end than the other. On the lighter end of the horizontal piece of wood is fixed a long piece of bamboo, at the end of which is a rude bucket. This is balanced, almost like a pair of scales. To work this water-lifter requires three or four men, one to stand by the bamboo which holds the buckets, and two men the other side to work the machine. As the man pulls down the bucket into the water of the well, the two men at the other side run up the inclined plane, then when the bucket is filled, they run down the inclined plane until they reach the ground, and the water is lifted up above the surface of the earth and poured out by the man who stands by the bucket upon the rice fields which are to be watered.

As you pass along the road, you see the different people taking their wares to market. Here is a man carrying umbrellas. These umbrellas, which cannot be opened and shut like our English umbrellas, are made of a bamboo cane and palmyra leaves. Here are men taking to the markets the pots and pans which are used in all the houses of the people for carrying and holding water, and for cooking purposes.

Here we see them crushing oil from the cocoanut in a large stone trough, into which is placed a heavy

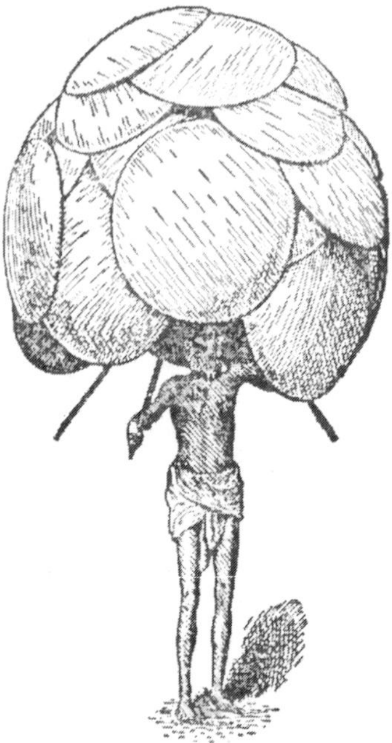

These Umbrellas cannot be Opened and Shut!

Taking Pots and Pans to Market.

piece of timber lying at an angle, and pressing upon the side of the stone vessel. Two bullocks, moving round in a circle, draw the piece of wood very tightly against the stone vessel, the oil is compressed out of the nut, and falls into a hollow below.

A TRAVANCORE WATERFALL.

"A ROUGH CART DRAWN BY TWO BULLOCKS."

As we travel along, we pass big reservoirs of water by the side of which are lively scenes. Here the people come in the morning to bathe, clean their cooking utensils, wash their bullocks, fetch water for their household purposes, and here especially can be seen the way clothes are washed by the

Crushing Oil from the Cocoanut.

dhobies (washermen). A large flat stone is the only article they use. Dipping the things in the water, the washerman swings them over his head, pounding them on the stone until they reach the cleanliness desired, and then they are spread out upon the ground to dry. This method of washing tears the clothes to pieces, and housewives find this their greatest torment, but the heat and the intense light of the sun bleach the clothes, so that though sometimes our clothes are delivered ragged, they are spotlessly white.

It is a common sight to see a mother bathing her

THIS METHOD OF WASHING TEARS THE CLOTHES TO PIECES.

child by the road-side, a woman doing up her hair in the open street, men and women squatting in rows, cleaning their teeth by the side of a tank, and the barber cutting hair in the open street, amidst crowds of passers-by.

Wandering about amongst all these people, in markets and in public places, are seen a great variety of beggars, wandering pilgrims, travelling ascetics, strolling musicians, conjurors, and snake-

THESE SNAKE-CHARMERS HAVE GREAT POWER OVER THE COBRA.

charmers. The snake-charmer appeals to one because of the deadly nature of the creature with which he deals. The cobra is one of the most deadly of all the snakes in India.

These snake-charmers seem to have great power over the cobra, but I believe that they render them comparatively harmless by irritating them early every morning, making the cobra bite something, and so discharge the poison from the poison glands and then they can be handled without fear for a

SNAKE WORSHIP FORMS PART OF THEIR RELIGION.

few hours. The snake-charmers hold the creature sacred, and in Travancore especially the cobra is treated with the greatest reverence—snake worship forms part of their religion—and around many houses, groves specially set apart for the comfort of these serpents are kept, and they are fed daily with milk and other delicacies.

But besides snake-charming, these conjurors

have many clever tricks. One is called the great Mango trick.

"Shall we show you a little conjuring, sir?" they come to the door and say.

The missionary's children, like all other children, say, "Oh, let us see the conjurors." He then spreads his slender apparatus on the verandah and commences his business. He swallows pins and needles, he produces berries and nuts of all kinds from nobody knows where, eggs and occasionally a pigeon or two appear; he swallows fire; from a little vessel which seems to hold half a pint he brings a fountain of water, but his great trick of all is what they call the Mango trick. Placing a little soil on the ground, he plants there a seed. Covering it up with a basket and a cloth, after making a few passes, he lifts up the basket, and in place of the seed there is a stem with two little leaves. After talking, as conjurors do, the basket is placed over this little plant. When lifted again, instead of a stem there is a little shrub. This process is again repeated, and the shrub grows, until finally there is built up before you a tree about two feet high, apparently perfect, with stem, leaf, flower and fruit.

The trees on the roadside as we pass are mainly banyan trees, and in some ways this is the most remarkable tree in the country. It is an immense tree, which lets a small gummy rootlet fall from its branches. These hang down, and on reaching the ground root themselves, and form a natural support to the larger branches of the tree. These branches, therefore, continue to extend, and form pillar-like stems all round the original trunk. The root drops are tough and elastic, they are much used for tent poles, cart yokes, and similar purposes. Bird-lime is made from the milky juice which abounds in every part of the tree. The leaves are used as plates by the people, and the fruit is occasionally eaten by them. Birds are very fond of it. There is one in South India whose measurements are as follows: Circumference of the parent trunk, sixty-one feet; width of the ground that is covered by tree and offshoots—east to west—two hundred and thirty-one feet; the same from north to south, two hundred and thirty-one feet; outside circular measurement of the whole tree, more than seven hundred feet. The tree is mentioned in Milton's great poem, "Paradise Lost," as being the great tree in the Garden of Eden to which Adam and Eve went after their disobedience. This is the way he describes it:

> So counselled he, and both together went
> Into the thickest wood; there soon they chose
> The fig-tree, not that kind for fruit renown'd,
> But such as at this day to Indians known

In Malabar or Decan spreads her arms,
Branching so broad and long, that in the ground
The bended twigs take root, and daughters grow
About the mother-tree, a pillar'd shade,
High overarch'd, and echoing walks between;
There oft the Indian herdsmen, shunning heat,
Shelters in cool and tends his pasturing herds
At loopholes cut through thickest shade.

THE PRINCELY PALM TREES.

The principal object in the landscape, as we travel from the frontier to the capital, is the immense number of palm trees. The palm trees, because of their immense value to mankind as giving food, raiment and many valuable objects of commerce, are called the princes of the vegetable world.

A great many kinds of palm grow in this country. The Areca palm (a small graceful stem with a crown of delicate leaves at the top) is a beautiful object. There is a country-saying that it is an arrow shot from heaven, and as we see its small, graceful stem, with its crown of delicate leaves waving by the breeze in the sunlight, it does have the appearance, not so much as a growth from earth, but as being shot into earth from overhead.

The Palmyra is a straight column, growing to the height of forty to one hundred feet, branchless, tall, with a stiff radiating head of fan-shaped leaves. Measured round the bottom near the ground, they will be about five and a half feet, round the top two and a half feet. It is the largest palm in India, except one called the false sago, and is certainly one of the most useful. It is a long time in growing, hence it is a common saying, that he who plants a palmyra tree never enjoys its fruits, but in favourable soil it yields in sixteen years. Another proverb is "Nattal ayiram vettal ayiram." "If you plant it, it could grow a thousand years; if you cut it down, it could last a thousand years." The uses of the tree are many. There is a poem in Tamil which tells us there are eight hundred purposes to which it may be applied. From this tree a man may store his grain, make his bed, furnish his provision, kindle his fire, draw his water, cook his

A Palmyra Climber.

Strolling Musicians.

food (in an earthen pot set on three stones), sweeten it if he chooses, and live day after day dependent on this tree. The Tamil poet says: "The areca palm, which must be cultivated every day, is the type of that friendship which must be strengthened daily. The cocoanut palm, requiring constant care in its earlier stages, is the emblem of that friendship which must be carefully guarded; while the palmyra tree is the emblem of those who, once friends, are friends for evermore, through adversity and prosperity."

The best known and every-day use of this palmyra tree is obtaining the juice or sap.

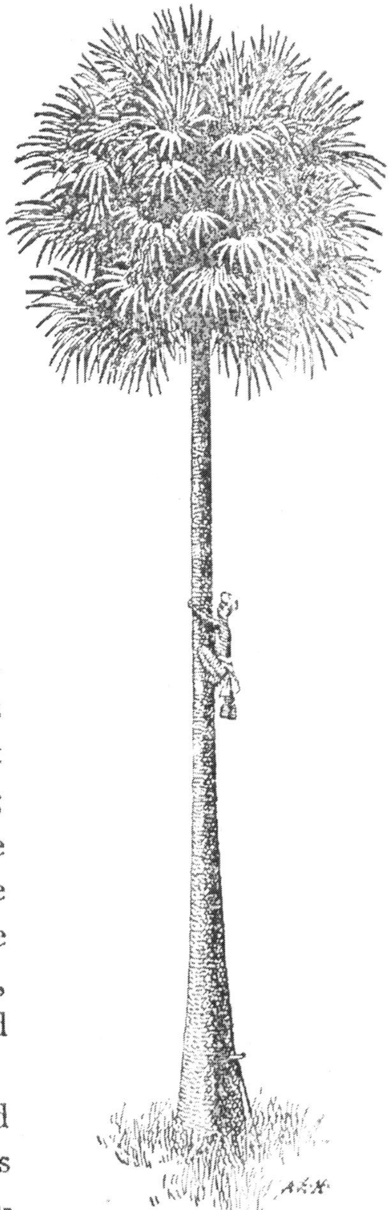

"To Climb a Tree sixty feet high is Hard Work."

This sap produces the palm wine or toddy, a drink which can be taken fresh or fermented, boiled down into sugar or distilled into spirits. In order, however, to get its riches, the tree must be climbed. To climb a tree sixty feet high without a branch to lay hold of is hard work, and to climb thirty or forty such trees twice each day is laborious. The juice is obtained by climbing and cutting the spadex on the young flowering branch. When this is cut the sap oozes out. The man then ties underneath a small earthenware pot, into which the juice flows. Every morning this is done, and every evening the tree is again visited, and the flowering branch cut, so that the sap may flow through the night. The sap which is obtained in the morning is sweet and refreshing. After sunrise it is intoxicating. Lime is generally used in the earthen vessel to prevent fermentation. After the climber has collected all the juice, his wife, or the female members of his family, boil it down till it becomes a coarse brown sugar.

It is from among these million hard-working, thrifty, palmyra climbers that nearly all our Christians come. Many of our converts have risen to occupy responsible positions in Government service.

Now we reach Trevandrum and must leave our bullock-cart for a boat to go north two hundred miles by canals and backwaters, i.e., inlets from the sea which run parallel with the coast. These backwaters are large lakes, a few miles from the sea, and in some cases so near the sea that you can see the waves dashing on the sand, and hear the roar of the waves as they break upon the shore. These lakes have been connected with one another by canals, cut by the Government, and a magnificent waterway of travelling can be had right through the land.

There are a great variety of boats, from the tiny

THE CANOE PADDLED BY A SINGLE BOY.

canoe paddled by a single boy, to the cabin boat propelled by sixteen rowers. We shall travel by what is called the Vallam. It is about twenty-five feet long, propelled by a man with a long bamboo pole, and he is sometimes assisted by another who rows with a paddle at the bow. There is a top made of bent bamboo covered with mat, and placing our luggage at one end of the boat, our mattress at the other, we start our boat journey at two and a half miles an hour. The palmyra has quite disappeared, giving place to the cocoanut tree. This is the land of the cocoanut. There are said to be ten millions in Travancore alone. They only flourish in the neighbourhood of the sea-coast, where their roots are almost laved in salt or brackish water. This forest of beautiful cocoanut palms, with their lovely crown of leaves and clusters of great nuts hanging from every tree, makes one not surprised that they called their land "Kerala," and say that Parasu Rama, when the land was reclaimed for him, brought this palm, planted it, and called it the beneficent tree of Heaven. There is no tree in India more useful. You get food, oil, light and medicine from the nuts, fire for cooking from the shells, coir for matting, roofing from the leaves, toddy and sugar from the stem. This tree alone gives a living to thousands.

As we pass along the coast we see strange logs of wood which the fishermen seem to use as boats. Do they go to sea on these craft? They are what you call "cattamarans." We call them "ketta marams," and that means tied wood. These fishermen are very brave men. I was visiting near a fishing village one day when a fleet of boats returned, and one boat was missing. "Have you a far-seeing glass, sir?" (i.e. a telescope) said one man. I had one, but looking all around I could see no boat.

They were very sorrowful, because they could not understand what had happened. The next day, at evening, news came that the boat had landed at a village thirteen miles away. The men were very exhausted, but they had caught and landed a shark ten feet long. What had happened was this. They had been fishing when this shark took their bait, hook, and all. Realizing that something big had got their bait, they wrapped their line as tightly round the prow of the boat as possible, sat still and awaited developments. The shark pulled them hither and thither; for fifteen hours they sat there without food until the shark was exhausted, and they towed it into the nearest village, dead.

CHAPTER III

AMONGST THE MOUNTAINS

I WANT now to take you a journey right up into the hills and mountains of Travancore. We must, therefore, leave our boat, and take to the bullock-cart again for about seventy miles. But before we start I want you to notice that beautiful vine, which is growing round and up the trunks of those large trees. Its leaves are a dark, rich green, and as the vine clings round the tree it makes the tree look almost treble its size. In and out of all these leaves there hang clusters of green berries, each berry about the size of a small pea. This is the pepper vine, and those berries, which become black and wrinkled after they have been dried in the sun, are exported in great quantities to Great Britain and other countries in the world.

Let us talk about pepper for a few minutes. How do you think our connection with India began? In this way. The Dutch people were in India before us, and they controlled the pepper trade. In the year 1599 the Dutch merchants raised the price of pepper against the English merchants from three shillings to six shillings and eight shillings per pound. The merchants of London did not like this, and they decided to form a Company to trade directly with India, and on October 1, 1600, the following ships sailed from England on their first voyage to India. These are the names of the first fleet.

	Men.	Tons.
Malice Scourge	200	600
Hector	100	300
Ascension	80	240
Susan	80	240
A Pinnace	40	100

This was the beginning of the East India Company. So the Malabar peppercorn was the beginning of British influence in India.

I want to take you into one of the highest mountains in Travancore, where, a few years ago, the missionaries built a small house, hoping to use it as a sanatorium in the hot season. It is a place called Muttukuly Vyal, and it means "The Pearl Pit Field." It is about five thousand feet above the sea level, and we shall have a very hard climb to reach the top. As we begin to ascend the hill we shall pass through some coffee and tea estates.

The coffee plants grow from two to four feet high. When in bloom the lovely white colour of the flowers

"THE TIGER WAS SOON SHOT."

"THE ELEPHANT FINDS HERE HIS GREAT HOME."

is a very pretty sight, and a coffee estate in blossom is equal in beauty to any apple orchard in England.

Tea is a shrub which grows to the height of three or four feet. It is planted on the hillsides on well cleared ground, in long rows. When they have reached about two and a half or three feet high, the tops of the shrubs are cut off, to increase the lower growth.

Picking the tea consists in taking the tender leaf shoots; these shoots comprise three to four leaves, inclusive of the tip or undeveloped leaf or bud. The tea picker gathers the very tip leaf, and the next two leaves below, taking care to leave one leaf on the stem or twig, in order that the new shoot for the next plucking may spring therefrom.

One man told me that one evening, coming down from his tea estates to the plains, just as the sun was setting he saw in the path along which he had to pass a tigress with two cubs. As he had no gun, and was alone, he climbed up the nearest tree. The tigress and cubs, which had some food they were devouring, spent the night around the foot of that tree!

We soon leave these tea estates behind, and then get right into the heart of the Indian forest.

With the exception of one little path there are no roads, and even this path is made out of a track made by elephants as they wander up and down the hills. The silence of these mighty hills, the great growth of vegetation, and the uncertainty as to whether on the path you will meet with wild beasts, is a most strange experience. For wild beasts are met with. One of our missionaries, a few years ago, was ascending this hill. He was walking in advance, his wife being carried in the chair, and two children in another chair behind her, with native men following, carrying all the provisions that they needed. As he turned a bend in the track he saw a huge form a few yards before him, and thought it was a cow. To his amazement it was a large tiger. He had the presence of mind to say to the man who was just behind him "Be still," and to his great relief the tiger looked at them and turned away and bounded into the jungle.

One adventure that I remember is of a tiger which had lost his way from the mountains, and had got amongst the villages in the plains. He did not seem to know how to get back, and so he "killed" his way along forty miles of road, until one morning he was found in the capital near the King's palace. Huge crowds were in a panic, and some Europeans with rifles went down to the scene. They found this tiger in a man's little field, where he had knocked a man down, and stood over him as if defying anybody to take the man away from him.

He was soon shot, but he had so mangled the man that the poor fellow died.

After climbing for six or seven hours we reach the place where the bungalow was built, and now we find ourselves on a broad plateau, extending all over the tops of these mountains, with miles and miles of untrodden forest. The loneliness, the eerieness, and the wonder of these solitary places of the world are indescribable. The climate

THE DEAD TIGER.

is cool, almost like an English spring, and for the first few days the feeling is one of wonder, amazement and delight. But after a few days the loneliness begins to pall upon one, and the uncertainty and apparent unsafety of the paths we have to walk in grows upon us. Sometimes a herd of elephants will be heard crashing through a jungle near; the bark of a stag upon a distant mountain, and at night time the occasional sound of wild dogs chasing an animal, and the cry of night birds.

I well remember one night, in this house, hearing the deep breathing and low growl of some great beast just near the door. It was a tiger which had come after a little calf that we had brought up. Mrs. Hacker said at once: "Oh, my dear, the babies." I got up and saw that all the doors were fastened, and that the babies were all right, and I am very glad to say that the next day that tiger was shot, and we were very relieved to get rid of it.

The elephant finds here his great home. They are wild in the forests, and in some places particularly abundant. They do not always remain in the same spot, but move about over large areas. There are about fifteen hundred to two thousand elephants in the forest of Travancore. The elephant is an exceedingly timid creature in his wild state. They go about in herds, and when they are together you can drive them as easily as driving a flock of sheep. But the most dangerous of them is what is called the "rogue" elephant. This is an old male elephant which, for some reason or other, has been driven out of the herd. He then has to wander by himself, and, as it is not good even for an elephant to live alone, he becomes morose, ill-tempered, and unpleasant. He will attack a single traveller or a party, if you are in his way, and it is astonishing to see, after he has done mischief, how quietly he can get away.

One day some coolies, who had been working on the neighbouring coffee estates, came rushing up to the planters, saying that an elephant had killed one of their boys. There were two planters in this house. Taking their guns they ran down to the riverside, and were told that while these men were sitting there taking their mid-day meal, this elephant rushed into their midst and struck the first he came to, hurling him into the river. The only sign of the boy was his waist cloth floating on the stream. They heard a noise in the jungle, and looking down, saw the elephant in a great rage dashing with his tusks and head at a tree. There seemed to be only two paths, and one planter said to the other: "You cover this path and I will cover that," and they sent some coolies to beat the elephant in their direction. There did not seem to be any escape for him, but he took the alarm, and, creeping most stealthily through the jungle, he got away like a mouse through a hole.

A very curious case of an elephant attacking a man occurred to one of our postmen once. He was carrying letters on his head, and climbing the hill along an elephant track, when he came face to face with a rogue elephant. The elephant knocked him down, and kicked him into a small hole on the side of the track. Then, gathering up all the leaves that lay about there, he threw them all over the man and buried him under them, and went away. Now, in all these jungle places there are a great number of ants—red ants, black ants, and brown ants. These were amongst the leaves in great numbers. Fastening upon the body of this man, they stung and stung him, until he was roused into consciousness, and crawled on to the path. Our letters not having come, persons were sent out to see where the postman was, and they found him terribly frightened, and in a half-dazed condition. After a few days' nursing, however, he was well again.

The next great creature on the hills is the bison. The colour of the bison is a dark coffee brown which deepens to black. The largest bull stands about six feet at the shoulder. They go in herds of some thirty or forty. One bull holds full sway in each herd, the younger animals do not dispute his authority. They never attack men, and move off at their approach into the forests. It is only when you shoot at one and wound him that you have to beware.

A European planter was brought to our Hospital some time ago with a great wound half-way down his leg. He had been out shooting, came across a herd of bison and shot the bull. The bull turned, saw the hunter, and having been wounded came rushing upon him almost like a flash of lightning. The planter shot again. The next moment the bull's horn had pierced him in the thigh. He fell between the bull's horns, and bull with the man in this strange position ran for about thirty yards, when the bison fell dead.

Tribes of monkeys wander about these jungles. One of the prettiest sights is to see a troop of monkeys leaping from tree to tree, chattering and playing as they go over the tree tops, and down the lower slopes of the hills with such wonderful agility. Up in the hills they have, of course, to earn their own living, by getting the fruits from the different branches of the trees, but down on the plains they are considered sacred; and especially in some parts of India, such as Benares, they are allowed to do very much as they like. They can go into the houses of the people, into the bazaars, and take the grain and the fruit, and sometimes become such a nuisance that they are even dangerous to life. They plunder fruit trees, and if the owner resists them by force, they come in larger numbers to overawe him. The result was that people living in Benares had to complain of the destructive acts of these monkeys. The British Government could not order them to be killed, as that would be against the religious feelings of the people, so they ordered part of the regiment there to capture all the monkeys they could, and, tying them together, put them in a train and deported them into some jungles a hundred or two hundred miles away.

In the forests these monkeys have many enemies. Their greatest is the python. There are a great number of snakes in Travancore—about

THE MONKEY'S GREATEST ENEMY IS THE PYTHON.

sixty-seven different species. The first question everybody asks, when they see a snake, is "Is it a poisonous one?" Most people say "Yes," and most people are wrong. There are only three

"THE IDOLS OF THE STATE HAVE A PROCESSION."

WRITING IN THE SAND AT SCHOOL.

A HAPPY TRAVANCORE CHILD.

deadly poisonous snakes in the whole country—the Cobra, (the hooded snake), the Russels-viper, with a thick body and a chain pattern running down the centre of its back, and the Krait, which has a bluish black body with narrow crosswise wide streaks or spots.

Rat snakes are common, and a very pretty little tree snake is a green one, sometimes found in bushes near the houses. The largest snake found in Travancore is the python, eighteen feet long, and as thick round as a man's thigh. These are the great enemies of the monkeys in the forests. It lies at the foot of a tree, coiled round very much like a log of wood covered with lichen. It lies perfectly motionless, and you may even tread on it before you know what it is. The older monkeys are keen enough to know the difference between a log and a snake, but the little inexperienced monkey will sometimes drop from the bough of a tree on to what he thinks is a piece of wood, and in an instant, like lightning, coil and coil in a thousand convolutions are wrapped round the little creature, life is compressed out of its little body, and he affords a meal for the python.

I should like to say a few words about the people that dwell on these hills. They are supposed to be the aboriginals of the country, who, having been driven into the hills by repeated invasions, have found their homes there. They are a most interesting little people; short in stature, thick-set and muscular in build, very simple in their lives. They live by climbing trees for honey, and gathering wild fruits of the forest, by making little clearings and cultivating a few simple roots. They are called "Kanikars," from "Kani," a clearing in the forest, and "Kar," the agent, or the clearer. They build their little huts on the branches of trees for fear of the elephants and wild beasts.

THEY BUILD THEIR LITTLE HUTS ON THE BRANCHES OF TREES.

They are truthful in life, and a very interesting people. After the advent of the coffee and tea plantations, the missionaries tried in various ways to get a mission amongst them, and we have paid some very interesting visits to these people and have built a church for the worship of God.

THE TEMPLE OF FIVE PORCHES.

CHAPTER IV

ROUND ABOUT THE TEMPLES

I SHOULD like to say "In and out of the Temples," but in Travancore these places are considered so holy that no European or low-caste man is allowed to go near even the gates of the temple, because their presence would be pollution.

There are innumerable temples in this little land. There are six thousand one hundred and fifty-nine temples devoted to the worship of the higher gods; three thousand two hundred and three temples devoted to the worship of the lower gods, and fifteen thousand small pagodas, sacred groves, sacred wells, and holy places. Besides these, there are innumerable shrines erected by the lower castes for demon worship. The higher gods are called Brahma, who is the Creator, Vishnu, who is the

Preserver, and Siva, who is the Destroyer, of the Universe.

There are no temples to Brahma, because the Brahmans are considered to be his temples, therefore they are the holy men of the country. When I say there are no temples to Brahma, I must correct myself a little, because near Ajmere there is one, and another in a place called Idor, and a very small shrine in the fort at Trevandrum.

Vishnu, the Preserver, is generally represented in a human form with four hands. One holds the club, the sign of conquest, the other the discus, a circular weapon something like a quoit, with jagged edges, with which it is said he cuts off the heads of his enemies. A third hand holds a lotus lily, which is an emblem of growth, development; and the fourth has a large conch shell. This has been adopted as the national emblem of Travancore, just as the rose, the thistle, and the shamrock have been adopted as the emblems of Great Britain. If you collect stamps you will see the shell on the Travancore stamps.

Siva, the third person in this triad, is represented in the character of the destroyer and regenerator, and he is called the great god, the auspicious one, and is greatly venerated in various parts of India.

We will visit first the great temple at the capital of the State. It is situated within a large wall, about a mile square, called the fort. In this fort is the Maharajah's palace, and all the buildings

SCULPTURE AT THE TEMPLE OF MADURA.

connected with the dwelling of His Highness, also a large number of Brahman streets, the houses occupied by the number of people engaged in temple service, and there is a large tank or reservoir, which is much used for bathing and purifying purposes.

Keeping this reservoir on the right hand we walk, and stand before the principal entrance to the temple itself. A handsome flight of stone steps leads to the entrance door, where there is a tall pyramidal tower, a hundred feet high. It has seven stories, and from the bottom to the top it is crowded with sculptured figures, some of them life-sized, and it has window-lined openings in the centre of its seven stories. Within is an enclosure, and inside that a circular building, the holy of holies, where the great idol is kept. It is a large figure of Vishnu asleep upon a coiled-up serpent. The town is named "Tiruvananthapuram" or "The abode of the holy serpent."

How do the people worship in this temple? First there is the high priest. He is supposed to be scrupulously clean and pure. For a term of six years he is supposed not to leave the temple or his own little house near it. During the day's services he is not allowed to touch, or to be touched by, any one. Even if a Brahman touched him he must go and have a fresh bath before he could carry on the services. He is assisted by some thirty-five assistants to the head priests. Then, besides, you have the light carriers, the musicians, the servants, the servant maids, the cooks, the water drawers, the flower garland makers, the hereditary singers.

But what *is* the worship? Service begins at four o'clock in the morning, when you hear the loud blowing of the conch shell. This means that the doors of the shrine are being opened. The priest enters the temple with his assistants, and after sprinkling water in front of the inner shrine, opens the door of the holy of holies.

Inside this place there is a golden image of the god, Vishnu. The other reclining image being too large to move, this one is taken out, and the old flowers, clothes and jewels, which were placed on it the previous night, are taken away. The image is then washed with water. An offering is made to it of fried rice, cocoanuts and plantain fruits. Then it is decorated with silk cloth, jewels and garlands of flowers. This closes the morning service.

At seven o'clock another priest pays a visit to the temple, and makes an offering of plantain fruits to the image. The flowers, and the water that has been used in washing the image, are given to the assistant priests, and these priests give a few petals of the flowers and a few drops of the water that has washed the image to all the worshippers who, by this time, have come to bow before the shrine. About eight o'clock His Highness, the Maharajah, will appear to render his homage to the idol, and then the image is again worshipped, adorned with flowers, lights are waved before it, it is fanned by assistants to keep him cool, and offerings of all kinds are made before him.

During this time a great number of Brahmans are fed at the expense of the State. At eleven o'clock a hundred and twenty Brahmans are fed inside the temple, then a small image representative of the god is carried on the head of a priest three times round, accompanied by temple music, while the people stand with hands clasped in adoration and closed eyes as the procession passes. From half-past twelve till five there is complete silence in the temple. In the evening the shrine is brilliantly lighted. The image is decorated with jewels, flowers, and silken cloths, the priests utter their hymns in praise to the god, the temple musicians with their flutes and drums and bells ringing, and the brilliantly lighted temple forms a great interest to all the people who have the privilege of entering the temple. Offerings of rice and sugar, and sugared cakes and cocoanuts, are made. This continues until about ten o'clock at night, when all the priests and servants leave the shrine.

Another form connected with their worship is the special processions which they make, and the dragging of the idol car. This idol car is huge and unwieldy, about forty feet high, weighing several tons, and is carved from top to bottom with characters in Hindu mythology. The idol is placed in

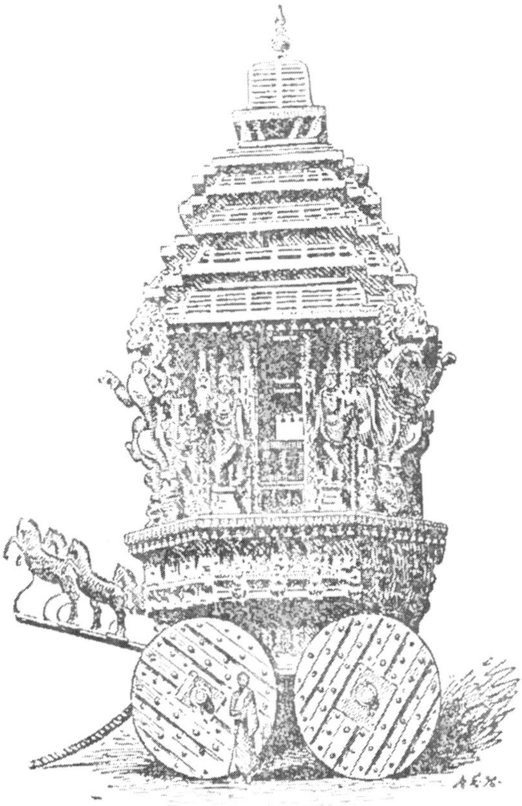

IN THE MONTH OF DECEMBER THE CAR IS DRAWN ROUND BY MEN.

the car with a priest as attendant, and, in the month of December, at one of the temples, crowds of people gather together, and the car is drawn round by men, who harness themselves to the ropes which are attached to it. It is very laborious work to draw it round the temple, and in olden times people thought it a religious merit to throw themselves under the wheels of this car, hoping by having their lives crushed out by this sacred car, they would at once enter heaven. The British Government have, however, stopped this, and in Travancore the people seem to be losing much of their zeal in this special form of service.

The idols of the State have a procession to the seaside, which is about two miles from the temple. After going round the temple the procession is headed by the Maharajah, unclothed, except by a waist cloth and followed by his personal attendants and bodyguard, by all the other male members of the royal house, by his soldiers with their arms, banners flying, band playing, the huge State elephants, and horses, richly caparisoned, all the Hindu officers of the State, the Sudras before the Maharajah, and the Brahmans behind him—all form a guard for the State idols, which are surrounded by all the high priests and servants connected with the temple. Roadsides are lined with people of all classes, and after reaching the beach, the idols are placed in a stone portico erected for the occasion. At sunset the images are solemnly bathed in the sea, after which the Rajah himself bathes, and the festival closes with the return of the gods to the temple about eight o'clock in the evening.

The temples connected with the lower gods are

THE GOD KRISHNA ASLEEP, GUARDED BY COBRA.

more public, and they are greatly resorted to by all classes of people.

The festival I am going to describe is held

at a place called Mundeikadu. Here there is a celebrated shrine to the goddess Bhagavati, one of the wives of Siva, the third person in the Hindu triad.

The people come from all parts of the country annually, in March, to pay their vows and make their yearly offerings. Beggars of all kinds are stationed at different intervals at about fifty yards apart. Here a blind man with several children, all in a pitiable condition; here a woman with a young child which seemed to have been born but a few hours; little children without a rag of clothing, covered with sores. It seems as if all the suffering creatures from the whole of Travancore had been gathered together and laid on the roadside. This continues for more than three miles, before we reach the place where the temple is situated.

Here, in front of this pagoda, and all around it, are crowded nearly twenty thousand people. Some are selling fruits, some cooking food, some offering to the idol, some killing fowls, sheep and goats, pouring out the blood before the idol, while there are shouts of those going to the temple, the braying of horns and the beating of tom-toms.

In front of the pagoda here is a boy paying some vow. He is brought so near that I could touch him by stretching out my hand. I see the men get a long piece of finely drawn wire, which they thrust through the boy's side. The boy screams, they shout to drown his cries, rude drums are beaten for the same purpose, and the boy is taken away, the people dancing behind him in apparent ecstasy.

Here you see a poor woman measuring her length on the ground round the temple, prostrating herself face downward to the ground, and stretching out her hands as far as she can she makes a mark with her hand. Then rising and placing her feet where her hands had made the mark, she again throws herself forward, and repeats that process. I see the woman two hours after, doing the same thing.

Here a man is lying like a log, and being rolled round the temple by his companions, heedless of the struggling, seething mass of people which were surging all around them. Such sights as these make one feel how sad it is that people should think that this kind of service is pleasing to our Heavenly Father.

It is amazing what curious vows these people make. There is a theory that a Hindu who aims at perfection ought to go through six courses of penance for twelve years. The men who follow these courses are called "Sanyasis," or ascetics.

This is one course. The ascetic eats, lives and is clothed in grass. One month he eats fruit only every third day. For the next month every sixth day, for another month every fortnight, and so on. They raise their arms until they are unable to lower them. The "Akasamuktis" (Sky-facers) hold their faces towards the sky until the muscles stiffen, and they live like that always. Others allow their nails to grow almost through their clenched hands. Another act is to sit in the midday sun with fires blazing all around.

A Hindu Ascetic.

One extraordinary case was reported a little time ago of one of these ascetics who turned up at a railway station, clothed in two hundred and forty pounds of iron chains and bands. He was on a pilgrimage to Benares. The stationmaster looked at him and decided that there was more iron than man there, and that, therefore, he could not be sent as a passenger, but came under the head of "Goods, by weight." He was accordingly weighed and booked as goods. But the iron under the tropical sun absorbed so much heat that the ascetic, who was an old man, was nearly dying before he reached his journey's end, and had to be continually sprinkled with water.

We have spoken of the worship of the higher gods, also of the worship of the lower gods, but there

A SHRINE IN THE FOREST.

are a great many people in Travancore who are not allowed to enter into any of the temples of the high caste people, and whose religion consists in the worship of demons or evil spirits. Amongst the poorer and more ignorant people, where life is hard, it is almost natural for them to say: "We do not know much about a good god, sir, but we do believe in a devil, because we have so much trouble."

Demon worship is most common in the south of Travancore. The spirits of wicked men who have been cut short of their existence in this world are supposed to have to spend the unexpired portion of their earthly life in unrest. At noon as well as at midnight, they are supposed to lie in wait to possess people.

The demon shrines are generally built out in the open, without any covering, a small obelisk about nine feet high. It is generally built of brick and whitewashed. In front of these are implements such as a dancing stick, and a trident. The demon priest or dancer, dresses himself in garments consisting of a high conical cloth cap, with tapes hanging down, supposed to form long shaggy hair; a jacket with embroidered representations of demons worked in red; and a pair of short breeches with bells all round the bottom. A thick club, ornamentally painted, having iron rattles or jingling brass rings at each end, is also held in the hand while dancing.

Now suppose we want to see a demon-worship

ceremony. There has been some epidemic in the village, and the people say "This is caused by a demon. We must, therefore, get a devil dancer to come and tell us what we are to do." The villagers then make a subscription, and arrange with the devil dancer to come on a certain night. Night

A VILLAGE TEMPLE.

is the best time. The officiating priest is dressed in appropriate ornaments and clothing, a band of musicians are engaged—these musicians generally have a tom-tom or a drum, a horn, a clarionet, and especially a curious instrument which is called the bow. It is a series of bells of various sizes fastened to the frame of a huge bow, and the strings are tightened so as to emit a musical note when struck. When all these preparations are made, and the dance is about to commence, the music at first is very slow. The dancer seems impassive; the music becomes quicker, and the movements of the dancer quicken accordingly. Five, ten minutes pass, when the music is as rapid as it possibly can be, and as the music becomes quicker and louder the excitement of the dancer begins to rise. Sometimes he drinks medicated draughts—music playing all the time, cuts and lacerates his flesh until the blood flows —music quicker all the time. He presses a burning torch to his breast, drinks the blood of the goat that has been sacrificed, then, as if he had acquired new life, he begins to brandish his staff of bells, and to dance with a quick unsteady step. Suddenly his body seems to distort itself, he stares and twirls round on his toes, as though supported by an unseen power, an awful sight, and it is then that the demon seems to have taken possession of him. Every bystander consults him as to what he is to do respecting the disease, the wants, the welfare of the relatives for whom he is making the offering. Everything that the man says is accepted as the will of the demon.

Many of the Christians who now belong to our Mission have been demon worshippers, and even after they have been Christians for many years the fear of these demons does not seem to be destroyed.

One of these demon priests, who came under the influence of Christianity, gave up his occupation, broke down his shrine, and became a Christian teacher. It is one of the sweetest memories of my missionary life. He came in contact with some of our Christian people, and was so struck by the serenity and calmness and peace that they had in their times of trouble, that he began to inquire the reason, and one of our dear old Christian teachers had great influence over him and finally brought him to the feet of Christ. He became a very earnest worker, and for fifteen years he has been doing splendid service.

CHAPTER V

AMONG THE HINDU CHILDREN

ALL the most famous stories in Indian books begin by relating how a high and mighty king and his beautiful and accomplished queen, reigning in splendour and prosperity over a happy and contented people, have everything that wealth can buy and heart desire, but they have one great sorrow because they have no children, and the story goes on to tell of the prayers they prayed, the vows they made, the sacrifices they offered, until their request is granted, and a child is given to them by the gods.

Here, coming from this village, are a man and his wife and their little boy, dressed in their best clothes, going to a festival. The man walks a few yards in front, the woman with the child in her arms follows. That is the custom, because in this country husband and wife do not walk side by side. We will give these people our salaam and speak to them, because they know the missionaries, and will not think that we shall do them any harm.

They are all dressed in their best, and especially notice the mother, covered with ornaments, around her ankles silver anklets, round her wrist and arms silver bracelets, and around her neck four or five necklaces of gold coins; jewels in her ears, and jewels in her nose.

Ask the mothei a question. "Which would you sooner lose, your jewels or your baby?" See her draw the little child closer to her, as without any hesitation she says, "Let all the jewels go, but let me keep my child." Now you can preach the Gospel to her. Tell her that she is one of God's children, that the sun shining in its strength over the fruitful fields, that the moon gleaming in silvery splendour through the forest trees, and upon the broad ocean, that the stars sparkling in the midnight heavens, these things are only God's jewels, and that we are His children, more precious to Him than sun, moon and stars. This is what Jesus Christ has told us.

They will open their eyes wide with wonder and astonishment and say: "This is wonderful talk, sir, can we believe it? It seems almost too good to be true."

Let us talk a little about the superstitions of an Indian home. The one thing that the Hindus believe in more than another, is that their very existence in this world, and their prosperity or adversity, is made by the influence of the time of their birth, and the star under which they are born. This is called astrology.

Every Hindu village has its village astrologer. When a child is born the parents mark the time carefully, and if they cannot accurately tell the time, they measure the baby's right foot, and from this the astrologer will tell whether the child is to be fortunate or unfortunate, happy or miserable.

Nothing can be done in the family without the astrologer. If the father has to make a journey, if the family have to arrange about a marriage, if their little boy is to go to school, if a purchase is to be made, the astrologer must be consulted, who consults the stars and gives them his advice.

Besides this, there is a great belief in omens and dreams. A Hindu rises in the morning troubled with a dream. If he dreams he sees a friend bathing in oil, that friend is about to die; if he dreams of a heap of fresh vegetables, a disease will come in the family. If he sees in a dream a quantity of unboiled rice, smallpox will come to his house. So the moment he rises from his mat after the night's sleep, he is depressed or elated by his dream.

Before he goes out of his house his first look must not be upon a broomstick, or a cat, or a widow, or a barber, or an oilmonger, or a heap of rubbish.

He then rises to go to the tank to bathe. If he should meet a cow, or a young girl, or a flower seller, he is pleased. If, after his bath, returning home, a crow should caw, or a lizard chirp, or a dog happen to touch him, he must again bathe. If, in the course of his morning meal, the light which burns before his idol should be accidentally extinguished, he is sure to have bad fortune.

If the father wants to get his daughter married, the astrologer has to compare the horoscope of the girl with that of the boy. If the horoscopes do not agree, he sometimes writes on three small bits of leaf, "First-rate," "Passable," and "Cannot." He takes these small pieces of palm leaf, and places them under the feet of the idol in the pagoda, and the priest takes one and gives him. If the word "First-rate" or "Passable" be picked up the marriage contract may be settled, but if "Cannot" is drawn, whatever may be the character of the proposed husband, the marriage cannot take place.

We will now talk about the children born and brought up in an Indian home. If it is a boy, there is great rejoicing all through the village. At night time you hear sometimes a great cry of joy uttered by women's voices, and you know that a boy is born in the village. If it is a girl, there is silence.

We will deal with the boys first. When the boy is four years of age, he receives his first lesson. A

Different Methods of Punishments in Non-Christian Schools.

Something to put in the Collection.

A Prince of Travancore.

"The Sudra came from the divine feet."

quantity of raw rice is placed in one vessel, and two measures of rice are placed on the other side of this vessel; a lamp is burning in the front of it. The boy is seated in front of the vessel, and the teacher takes a gold coin and writes upon the boy's tongue the name of "Ganapatha," which is supposed to be the god which presides over education. He then takes the boy's first finger on the right hand, and makes him write the name in rice—that is the boy's first lesson.

When the boy is between five and six years of age he is taken to the village school. Now in these days, when Western methods are being adopted, blackboards, books and slates, white-washed walls, and pictures are common necessaries in a modern school. But I want you to see what a real Hindu village school is.

Here is a little canal running from a reservoir through a village. On the bank of this canal stands a little building, about twenty feet long by fifteen feet broad. The framework consists of four rough palmyra posts. The thatch is of cocoanut leaves, and a mud wall about five feet high runs between these palmyra pillars. The floor is swept clean and washed well with cow-dung and water. In one corner of this building is a heap of sand, and hanging from the roof are bundles of palm leaves which the children write upon. Those who are learning first write with their fore-fingers in the sand, making the letters. Those who have learned their letters, write upon palm leaves with an iron pen, which they call a writing nail. Those who are advanced students are learning by heart Tamil and Sanskrit verses. The old schoolmaster looks very drowsy and lazy, and he does not interfere with his scholars much. Then they have an arithmetic lesson; it is a learning of the multiplication table. One boy says "Eight times nine, seventy-two," and all the rest shout this at the top of their voices, and in this way they go on until they reach twelve times twelve, and the din and noise make you wonder how it is possible a boy can learn at all.

Just a word on the punishments teachers inflict upon the boys at school for disobedience. I am speaking now of those schools which are untouched by Western methods. The worst of all is one which is called "kothandam."

A pupil upon whom this was practised thus relates his case. He says, "I had thrown a stone at a mango tree in mischief, and I was a fool to do this, but the owner of the mango tree saw me, and ran after me to the school. The schoolmaster mercilessly beat me, and finally he declared that he would inflict upon me the punishment of kothandam. There was a short rope hanging from a crossbeam in the middle of the school. Sand was heaped just below this rope, and all the available iron pens were planted in that sand with the sharp points upwards. My waist cloth was tucked up to the waist, so that the blows might fall upon the bare skin, and three of my fellow-scholars lifted me up bodily, and made me take hold and cling to the rope with both my hands. I was advised to hold firm, for if I dropped down my feet would be pierced by the points of the iron pens below. Then that merciless brute of a teacher flogged me furiously with his cane. After the ninth blow I dropped down and fainted away, with my left foot pierced." I am glad to say these brutal punishments are now passing away.

Some of the stories they read in their school books are most interesting, and are great favourites with all the Indian people. But the ordinary bazaar books, consisting of short stories, have a charm of their own. I will give you two or three.

"The Thief and the Cocoanut Tree."—A certain man owned a grove of cocoanut trees. One day, sitting in his house, he saw a thief climbing one of his trees. Running out of his house he came to the foot of the tree, and the thief, seeing him, descended. They met at the foot of the tree: "Hullo," said the man, "what are you doing up my tree?" "Please, sir," said the thief, "I have a little calf, and I wanted some grass for it." "Oh," said the owner, "grass on the top of a cocoanut tree! You cannot find grass on the top of a cocoanut tree." "No, sir," said the thief, "That is the reason why I came down," and before the man recovered from his astonishment, away ran the thief.

Another curious story: A certain man went to the temple and prayed for a manifestation of the goddess. She appeared with a thousand faces on the right, a thousand faces on the left, a thousand faces before, and a thousand faces behind, but with only one pair of hands. Upon seeing this vision the man broke out into uncontrollable laughter, and the goddess, enraged, said, "Why this irreverence?" "I beg your Highness's pardon, I could not help it, because a thought came into my mind, and I could not help laughing. It was this—if ever your Highness had a cold, how would you wipe all those noses with one pair of hands."

There are scores of such stories as these, and the boys have really a good time.

What about the games these boys play? Do they play games?

Yes, the boys are very fond of all sorts of games, and it is a very strange thing that many of the games are similar to those in Western lands. Marbles they are very fond of. A game something like our stag and hounds, a rude kind of football, and a kind of mimic fighting with staves, form the most of their active games, but they are now—especially those who are having an English education—taking greatly to lawn tennis, badminton, football and cricket.

If the baby is a girl, how is she dealt with ?

I should like to say here first of all that the little girls are loved very dearly by their parents. The customs of the country are very hard upon the girls, but the natural affection of father and mother for their little girl is as strong as it can be in any country. I should be very sorry to say anything unkind or untrue about the Hindu fathers and mothers, because I know how very deep is their affection for their children. Besides in India some of the sweetest stories in all their books are those relating to the beautiful conduct of the women of this land, and certainly there is a grace and a sweetness about many of the women. I have a great admiration for the quiet, graceful, simple lives of many of the Hindu women.

But when all that is said and done, there is no denying that the lot of the Hindu girl is not a happy one. When she is born there is no rejoicing. She is not sent to school like her brother. She is a little old woman all too soon. Sometimes a child of six years goes through the marriage ceremony with an old man. At four years of age she is set to household work, and at five the little child lays her toys aside. Instead of a little girl playing about she has either so many household duties to do to help her mother, to sweep and cow-dung the floor, go to fetch water from the well in vessels according to her size, carry about the baby, almost as big as herself, on her hip, and not often do you see her free, happy, innocently playing. When they get time they have their little games. One game—I think they call it "knuckle bones"—is played with five stones, throwing them up and catching them on their knuckles; then games with little red seeds, passing them from one vessel to another. They must have their dolls. These they make from a big flower which we have in India. It is a kind of hibiscus, of the marsh-mallow family, and bears a large red or fawn coloured flower. The petals of this flower make a very pretty cream coloured or red fluffy skirt. The calyx of the flower makes the head, two pistils poked into the calyx make very nice arms, and the ends of the pistils make the hands, and there you have a dear little doll. They are fond of swinging, and of making little waggons. They have pleasant little singing and dancing

A LITTLE OLD WOMAN.

games, and some of their dances and songs are very pretty indeed.

Altogether, and in spite of the apparent hardships, young girl life is fairly happy. But her trouble soon begins. Ten is about the average age when a Hindu girl is married. Then she is either the mistress or the drudge of a household, and it is injurious to her in every way, for she is unequal to the responsibilities of being the mistress, and she is unequal to bear the strain of being the drudge. Or perhaps she is a second wife, and has to hold the balance between her step-children and her own. A few of them are taught to read, but they have not many books in the native tongue, and even if they had, they are not very fond of reading. A short course of music is taught to them, and they learn a few of the temple slogams, and some of the poems connected with the history of Krishna.

SWINGING BABY TO SLEEP.

The great trouble for these girls comes should it happen for the husband to die. A little girl of six is sometimes married by a religious ceremonial to a young man of eighteen. If this young fellow should die, this little girl is condemned to widowhood for ever. This is one of the greatest sorrows of the Hindu family.

After the husband's death, when several ceremonies are performed, the child widow is deprived of all her jewels, she is given a white cloth instead of a coloured garment. She is enjoined to have one meal a day, and that a light one. She is not allowed to mix with other women whose husbands are alive, because she is deemed to be a very sinful woman. She must sit in one corner of the house repeating some of the sacred names of Vishnu. She cannot play with her companions, and the bitterness of the whole thing is this, that her very parents at first scold her, saying that she must have been a very great sinner in her former birth, and now she has brought sorrow upon herself, and disgrace upon their family. It is a pitiable story, and it is no wonder that in the old times some women preferred to die with their husbands rather than live such a life.

I am glad to say that amongst the Hindu peoples themselves, there is growing a strong desire to break through the evils of some of these customs, and with the growing light that is coming amongst them, through the influence of Christian thought

IDOLS IN A VILLAGE SHRINE.

On the Road in Travancore.

and life, we may hope that many of these disabilities will pass away, and the Hindu woman will rise, because the sweetest, truest influence that makes for the wealth of the country is a noble womanhood.

CHAPTER VI

HOW THE RINGDOVE MET THE KING

THERE are three most interesting stories of how the Gospel of Jesus Christ came to India. I might tell you first how a little band of Christians in Palestine, in the early history of the Christian Church were driven out by persecution and travelled up the Red Sea and over the Indian Ocean till they found a home and protection in this land. I might tell you the story of how these Christians were supposed to be the disciples of the Apostle Thomas, and how it is related that having found favour with the Indian kings, they settled on the west coast of India on the borders of Travancore, how they multiplied and became a great people, and how it is said they actually had a little Christian kingdom with a king of their own at the time the Gospel was being preached in England.

I could tell you how they lost their first love, until they became almost a dead Church. This is a sorrowful story, because, if this Church had done its duty in the early centuries we might not be obliged to preach the Gospel at the present time.

Then I might tell you how in the beginning of the sixteenth century, when Spain and Portugal were in the height of their power, the Roman Catholics came with the power of the conquerors behind them, how they found this little Syrian Church and began to persecute it, and break it up, and tried to destroy it; how that great Jesuit Missionary, Francis Xavier, worked on the south coast of India; how, under his advice, the Office of the Inquisition was set up at Goa, and how for one hundred and fifty years the Hindus at frequent intervals saw Christian people burning one another at the stake, just as they did here in the bad old times, and all this done in the name of our dear Lord and Master.

The story I want to tell you now is how the ringdove met the great king, how their names were changed, and how the great king became the "Pearl of Scripture" and the ringdove became the "Messenger of God." That sounds almost like a fairy tale, and yet it is truer than any fairy tale can be, and more lasting in the blessing that it has brought to the people at Travancore.

Once upon a time, a little more than a hundred years ago, there lived in the very southern portion of Travancore a man named Maharasan, which means the great king. This seems a great name to give to a poor man, but in India people often give great names to very little things. There is a little native boy playing in the dust in the streets. He looks very dirty and unkempt, but if you ask his name you are told he is called "The Divine King," or the "Lord Shiva," or the "Pearl of God." These are some of the great names they give their little children, and then in order to take away the evil consequence, they call their children in their homes by little bad names, such as "The little pup." Maharasan was not in what they call the caste-system. He had to stand at distances from high-caste people, because he would pollute them; he could not walk along the same streets or enter the same villages, use the same wells, bathe in the same tanks, or worship the same gods. But he was an intelligent, fairly well-educated man. He and his wife and children lived in a small house upon the borders of rice fields. They had been frugal, industrious, and according to Hindu custom, pious people, and around their dwelling-place was a garden filled with palmyra and cocoanut palms, bananas and other garden produce, and near by some rice fields of his own. He was greatly honoured for his good character, and his family was considered to be among the most respectable and well-to-do of his class. But although he had as far as possible all that ministered to his comfort—wife, sons, land and a home—his mind was filled with great distress and sorrow because he felt he was not in harmony with the Divine Power.

His soul longed for peace and for a vision of God.

He could not get this at his demon shrine, he was not allowed to enter the temples devoted to the worship of the higher gods, but he heard that three hundred miles away, at a place called Chitambaram, there was a great sacred temple dedicated to the god Shiva, where he might find what he desired.

So one day, summoning his wife and children and other members of his family, he said—

"I am going on a pilgrimage until I reach my lord Shiva's temple at Chitambaram." This news struck great distress into the hearts of his family. "If you take this terrible journey," said his wife, "I am afraid we shall never see you more. The dangers of three hundred miles on foot, through ways infested by robbers, by Thugs who make a religious profession of strangling people by the way, are so great that we beseech you, pray to your god here and do not leave us." "This I have resolved," said Maharasan, "and I feel impelled by an inner voice which says 'Do what I command,' and we must obey the highest in us."

So Maharasan, clothed as a Hindu ascetic, with a rosary of beads around his neck, a staff in his hand, smeared on forehead and arms and chest with sacred ashes, took leave of his people and began his journey of three hundred miles, visiting scores of shrines by the way, resting at night under the shade of some trees, until at last he reached the famous temple at Chitambaram. And when he reached there his feeling was: "Here at last, in this sacred shrine, in the presence of these holy men," he said, "here surely I shall be guided in my quest after the vision of God." Very devotedly worshipping and offering on the shrine all the money he had, praying for peace, he was greatly disappointed when he saw the greediness of the priests, the godlessness of the vast crowds, the dancing girls, and the unspiritual nature of the ceremonies that were performed. His heart failed within him as he said: "I have travelled far, enduring severe hardship. How can I meditate on God in the midst of these abominations. Here I cannot obtain eternal bliss. What shall I do, where shall I go?"

Weary, he lay against one of the stone pillars of the temple, and falling asleep saw a vision in his dream.

An elderly man with a staff in his hand said, "You will find no peace here; return to your village, and I will show you the way in which you should walk." So saying he appeared to strike Maharasan with his staff. He at once awoke and started towards the south early in the morning. On the way home he had to pass through a town called Tanjore. In this town there resided a distant relative who had become a Christian. Maharasan attended the services, and he heard how One who was rich beyond our conception of what riches mean, became poor beyond our conception of what poverty means, that we—by His poverty, through His sinless life, by His cruel death and His victory over the grave—might be made the sons of God. As though scales had fallen from his eyes, these truths shone into his soul and he felt that this was the message he needed.

After the service was over, the missionary, a European, saw him standing at the door in his pilgrim dress, and said, " You are a stranger here, what do you seek ? " " I am seeking for the vision and the peace of God," was the reply. " Come to my house," said the missionary. He went, and studied there for five or six weeks, and the influence of God's spirit worked upon him so mightily that he gave his heart to Christ and became a consecrated soul. He then asked for baptism, and was baptized in the name of " Vethamanikan," which means the " Pearl of Scripture."

On account of his long absence, his wife and relatives supposed that he was dead and called in the astrologers, who confirmed their thought, and the result was great mourning in the house of Vethamanikan. But suddenly, one night he appeared at home, and great was the joy of all his relatives

Shushindrum Pagoda.

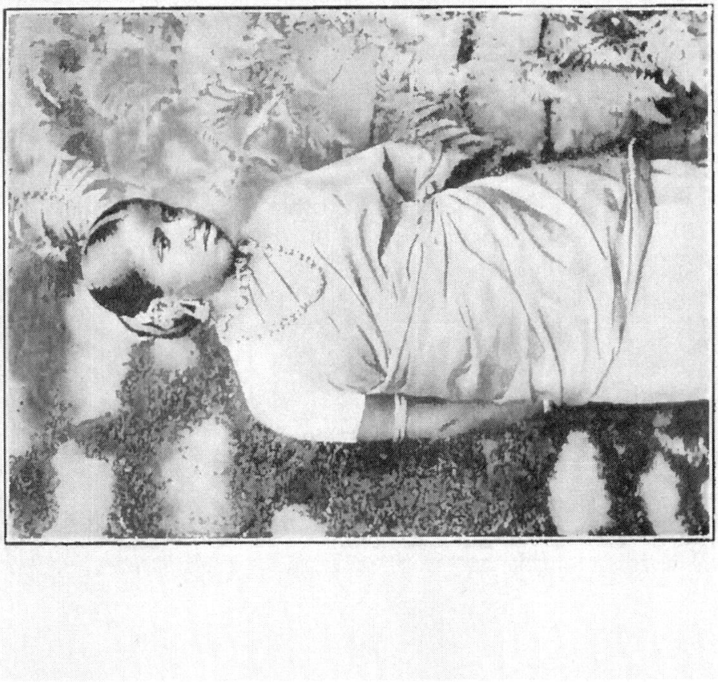

A Woman of Travancore.

A Group of Travancore Missionaries.

Boy and Girl before and after becoming Christians.

at seeing one almost alive from the dead. When the first astonishment was over, his wife said: "Where are the sacred ashes? Where is the holy water from the temple? Where are the other things which tell of the success of your adventure? Your rosary is gone—you are not smeared with sacred ashes, and your countenance seems to have changed!" "This," said Vethamanikan, producing the Bible and some tracts and books which had been given to him, "these are the divine pearls I have gathered on my journey. Here is the holy gift of the Lord of all the world." As they had never seen paper before, they were struck by great astonishment, and he then explained to them the new teachings he had received; how the Eternal Father had sent His Eternal Son, Jesus Christ, to live for us, to die for us and to save us from our sins, and he there preached the Gospel to his own relatives as far as ever he knew it, and gathering his family round him, he knelt in prayer that the Divine Light might shine upon them and all that called them friends.

About this time, William Tobias Ringeltaube (his surname means "Ringdove"), who had lived in Poland in Europe, had a great desire put in his heart to serve Jesus Christ in the mission field. He came to England, and, accepting service under the London Missionary Society, was sent to India.

After much uncertainty as to where his station should be, and while studying the language at Madras, and praying for guidance, one day an elderly man called at the Mission bungalow and told him that in Travancore, where he came from, there were two hundred people around about his village who greatly desired to become Christians, and begged him to come at once.

RINGELTAUBE (RINGDOVE).

Mr. Ringeltaube felt this to be like Paul's Macedonian cry, "Come over and help us," and at once made up his mind to go to them. The old man was Vethamanikan, and what had happened to bring him to Madras was this:

Vethamanikan in Travancore had been preaching to his family and friends. His heathen neighbours began to persecute him. The Gospel news, which had been spreading, reached the house of the royal family. The rulers, hearing of his work, determined to ruin him and drive him out of the country.

This persecution became so terrible that he felt he must sell all his little property and leave Travancore for ever. But one day, while reading and praying, he broke out into prayer as follows: "O Lord, when I worshipped idols which have no life, thou didst reveal Thyself to me, a great sinner, Thou didst pass by the rich and learned and chose me to be Thine. Now teach me what I should do. Is it Thy will that the light which has begun to shine here should now be quenched?" While he was praying this prayer, there was borne in upon him the irresistible conviction that he must not sell his field, but there establish God's kingdom. He therefore set off to walk to Tanjore again to see the missionary. As soon as this missionary, Mr. Kohlhoff, saw Vethamanikan, he said: "God has had mercy on you; He has sent a missionary called Ringeltaube, who is now learning Tamil, and when he has made sufficient progress in the language he will go to your village. But he is now in Madras."

"I must go and see him," said Vethamanikan, and at once started on foot for another two hundred mile journey, where for the first time these two men met. It was in this way the Great King met the Ringdove, and together they founded the Travancore Mission.

On April 25, 1806, Ringeltaube passed through the Pass of Aramboly, where we entered Travancore in our second chapter. This was the first time a

European Protestant missionary had ever crossed into Travancore.

Over all the land, as far as possible, Ringeltaube and Vethamanikan preached the Gospel of the Kingdom. Sometimes they were depressed, but they had a foundation of courage which helped them to bear with all difficulties.

In the year 1816, after nine years' faithful service, Ringeltaube's health failed him and he left the country. He solemnly ordained his native preacher Vethamanikan and urged him to be faithful. What happened to him cannot be correctly stated. One letter was from Ceylon, another from Malacca. It is reported that he was murdered by natives in the Malayan Peninsula, but nothing can be fully known. The general feeling is that he died of some disease upon board ship and that he found a grave in the mighty ocean. He sleeps in a nameless grave, but his soul was in God's hands, and whether he was buried in the mighty ocean or killed in Malayan jungles, or laid to rest in earth's quiet bosom in some strange land, his soul is in the hands of God, but his works will follow him for generations.

CHAPTER VII

"AT THE FEET OF THE TEACHER"

IN India the caste system says, "A boy who is born in a poor position must remain there; it is the religious duty of the high-caste man to keep him down." Therefore education is denied him, and reading or hearing the religious book is forbidden to the Sudra, even although he is in the caste system.

The people who are classed as out-castes in India had no real friends until Christ's people came to them. Till the middle of last century slavery existed in Travancore, the lower classes were attached to the land and transferred and sold with it. You could buy a man for sixteen rupees and a woman for ten. The first step towards improving their condition was due to the spread of Christianity amongst them by the labours of the missionaries. Education also spread and thus paved the way beyond all else for their betterment. Then the missionaries worked for the abolition of slavery, and in 1853 the Rajah liberated all Government slaves. In 1855 he abolished all kinds of slavery in the State, and from that time their conditions have been steadily rising.

It is touching to hear the fathers and mothers say, "Our day is over, but educate our children, for we pray that they may have more enlightened lives than we have had." The missionaries have been obliged to take up the education of the children, and we have nearly four hundred schools with fifteen to twenty thousand children under instruction, besides a large College at Nagercoil, where Christians and Hindus receive a good Christian training. The effect of this teaching is seen through the country in the growth of Christian influence. The following story will explain my meaning :—

Guru Patham ("at the feet of the teacher" is the meaning of that name) is a Christian of about twelve years' standing. By trade he is a wood-cutter. A short time since a Hindu met him and said, "I know you are a Christian, and with all your faith in Jesus Christ will you go to a certain wood and cut down a tree in the Demon Grove?" (these demons, according to the native notions, having their dwellings in groves). The Christian man said he would as he was challenged, and taking his axe went to the supposed sacred spot.

A crowd of demon worshippers had gathered round to witness the scene, evidently expecting some evil would happen to him. The man knelt down and prayed, then arose and began to chop. When he was about half-way through the tree, he fell down, half-fainting with excitement and exhaustion. The demon devotees set up a shout and running to a pagoda asked the Brahmin priest what they should do. The priest gave them some sacred ashes and told them to smear him with them quickly and make him say that he was quite defeated by the demon. But the man recovered, and seeing these ashes upon him went to the river and bathed—then he came back and completely cut down the tree. With this poor Christian man, who had only a few years ago emerged from demon worship into the light of the Gospel, this was a real trial of faith.

I HAD TO TRAVEL IN A BULLOCK-CART ALL NIGHT.

Some time ago, when visiting some churches many miles from my house, I had to travel in a bullock-cart all night. Just as the daylight was coming in on the Sunday morning, I got out of the cart and sat by the road side making a cup of coffee. The road I was travelling ran through some jungle and there was no house near. While I sat there a little boy about ten years of age came along the jungle path. When he saw my cart standing in the road he stopped suddenly and shouted in a frightened tone, "Shall I come down the road, sir, or must I go through the jungle?" He thought that I was a high-caste man and that he would get a severe thrashing if he came on further without giving notice, because his going near him would pollute the high-caste man. "Come down the road, my boy," I said, and he came, a bright-faced little boy. After some talk, I said, "How far is it to Kattarakari?" He said, "About five miles, sir," and then his little face brightened as he said, "I am going there, sir."

"What for?" I asked. "I am going to that little church for prayer, sir." Dear little fellow, he had started away from his home long before light, walked through the jungle for some miles in order to be at the church for Sunday services at seven o'clock.

Here is a story of how a boy may rise. A Christian man named Porothudian ("a servant of patience") and whose wife's name was Saral, had two sons, one whom they named Sattianesan ("the friend of

A SIVITE GURU.

SCHOOLMASTER.

A HINDU PUNDIT.

truth"). This boy developed a remarkable gift for learning. He passed rapidly through the schools, and learnt as much English as it was possible to learn in the schools of the country. He then took his Bachelor of Arts degree at the Madras University. After his return to his native country, his highness the Maharajah gave him an appointment in one of the courts of our land. He became the first Christian magistrate, and for many years he has dispensed justice over high and low with integrity and impartiality, winning honour for himself and the Christian name.

One of my boys named Stephen, who had received a fair education in our Mission School, went to Ceylon a few years ago as conductor on a tea estate. After he had been there some years his employer wrote to me: "Send me a dozen more men like Stephen. I have found him all I wish—honest, industrious, and dependable."

Even amongst the highest and wealthiest classes in India only a very few girls are taught to read and write; while amongst the very poor the idea of teaching them is ridiculous. "To educate a girl is like putting a torch in the hands of a monkey," is one of their proverbs. The monkey might set fire to a forest, and an educated girl would do more harm than good.

A Brahmin gentleman was once asked, "What do

you think a woman ought to know?" His reply was: "She ought to know two things only—First, the way to the market to buy things for the house, and second, the way home again; that is quite enough for women."

A Hindu teacher was once requested to teach Tamil poetry and literature in one of our schools. At first he utterly refused, because, said he, "If you educate girls they will not become obedient wives." "Look at my wife," he said; "she cannot read and can only count up to ten, but that is quite sufficient for her."

The result of all this is that even amongst the higher castes, out of over a hundred women only four are able in any way to read or write. That being the case amongst the higher castes, you may imagine what the conditions of the poor people must be. Before the Gospel came to this land there was none to help them, and they lived their hard lives and died their obscure deaths without a ray of God's love to brighten their unhappy lot. Many of them were slaves. A few years after the missionaries had been in Travancore this thing happened—

One morning, about ten o'clock, a missionary was reading on his verandah and preparing for his church services, when he saw a little girl about ten years of age come in timidly at his gate and then rush with all possible speed to the place where he was sitting. Falling at his feet and almost fainting, she cried, "Oh, sir! save me, save me!" "Whatever is the matter?" asked the missionary, and the little girl, sobbing, said: "I am a slave, sir, and my master is unkind and cruel and wicked. Save me from him!" "I will do what I can," said the missionary, and calling his wife they took the little girl into the house, gave her food and a good bath, some clothes to wear, and tried to comfort her. Next day, early in the morning, a stout, pompous, proud caste man, who was a large landowner living about five miles away, came stalking up to the missionary's house. As soon as he entered he said in a loud voice, "You have here a runaway slave of mine, and I want her immediately." "Yes," said the missionary, "it is true. A little girl came here yesterday very much terrified. She is here resting, and you have treated her so cruelly that she needs care and attention. Please let her stay with us." "I want my slave," he replied. "But," said the missionary, "I will buy her of you. I will give twice the market value of her, and will pledge myself to treat her kindly." "I don't want your money, I want my slave," was the stern reply. Nothing would move him, threatening, entreaties, offer of compensation, were of no avail, and it was heart-breaking work when they were obliged to give up this little girl again to the hands of her wicked and cruel master. Those bad times are all gone. A few years after this slavery was abolished in this country, and now the poorest classes are free, and such scenes as these can never happen again. This is one thing done for the poorest classes in the land, which the Gospel has made possible.

One of the first things the missionaries did was to establish girls' schools, and these have worked wonders amongst the Christian girls; and the Hindu Government, following the missionary example, have now established girls' schools in many parts of the country, and the education of girls has now become quite a feature in the land. "As might be expected," says a high Hindu official, "the missionaries were the first to establish girls' schools." They organized boarding schools for the children of Christian converts, and the object of these schools was to give plain instruction united with a Christian moral education.

At the present time we have now in our Mission schools for girls in every district, and six thousand girls under instruction. These efforts are quite recognized now as great things by the Government, and in their reports they tell us that foremost amongst those who are able to read and write stand the Christians; the Christian community in respect of both sexes are the best educated in the state.

Native Christian women and girls are not only first, but far ahead of all other religions in education, so that while amongst the Hindus, ninety-six out of every hundred are unable to read, one in every six of Christian women are able to read and write. I should like you to remember this, because it is a proof of a very great fact in Christian history, that in whatever country the Gospel is honestly received, the first and chief blessing that comes from it, is that which raises girls and women.

I want now to take you right through a little Christian girl's life as far as possible. When a little girl baby is born in some homes, even where there is poverty, or several girls already, the child is not looked upon as a punishment to the parents, but as a gift from God, from their heavenly Father, to be trained for His service. Here is a difference at the very start of that little life. Mothers who have been educated sew neat little frocks for the baby girl, call her pretty endearing names, and teach her to lisp the name of Jesus as soon as she can speak. The first place Baby must go to is to the church to be baptized, and then she must be brought to see the missionary's wife. A sweet little Christian name is given to her; instead of Issakee or Kali, the name of some cruel goddess, the name of Pakkiam, that is "Happiness," or Vethapu, "Flower of the Bible," is given to her.

When the little daughter is five or six years of age, she is not betrothed in marriage like the little Hindu girls, but is sent to the village mission school close at hand. She goes to the Sunday School on Sundays, and at the public services when she is little she is allowed to sit by her father, for you know in that land in all churches, the women and the girls sit on one side of the church and the men on the other. From five years old to ten she is educated in the village school. When the girl is ten or twelve years of age, another step comes into her life, if she belongs to Christian parents. Perhaps you think she is surely going to be married now, as would be the case of the little Hindu girl. Not at all. She is seeking admission in the missionaries' Boarding School for Girls. But, you say, that is the age when the heathen girl is taken away from her day school and has to be secluded in her home.

GIRLS GRINDING CORN.

This is the time our Christian girl leaves her home for the first time and goes away from the surroundings of heathenism which are about that village and comes into a Christian home where Christian influences surround her, where she is learning daily of Jesus and His love, learning her Bible and its blessed truths and is preparing herself to be a light bearer to her own home and village.

When she is fifteen years of age you say surely she must be leaving school now. No—when she is fifteen years of age she begins to learn how to work embroidery or lace. This is an industry that is taught them by the missionaries' wives, which gives them employment for their leisure hours, teaches them to do very fine needlework and enables them when they leave their school for their home, to earn a little money for themselves, which they save for the time of their marriage, or give to the mother to help in the expenses of the family. This embroidery and lace industry has been of great service to the Christian girl. They have excelled in the work and it has, at most of the Exhibitions in India, been much admired, and taken the gold medal for excellence.

In this way we keep the girls in the Christian school till they are seventeen or eighteen years of age, and she leaves the school fully equipped for all the duties of life, and above all has the foundation of a true and happy life because she has found as her Saviour, Jesus Christ. What a difference this makes needs to be seen in order that you should really understand it. You can see it in her face and bearing. There is a sparkle of intelligence in her eyes, a bright happy look with no fear in it. It is the light of Jesus Christ shining in her and through her. As the years pass there is growing up in the Christian congregations a new womanhood, not entering upon the cares of life before the proper time. Visitors who have come to see us, say that even as they walk along the streets they can tell by the bearing and serene contentment of the educated Christian women, which is the Christian woman and which the heathen. Some of these girls marry very happily, the teachers or catechists connected with our Mission, and become helpful and devoted fellow workers with their husbands.

I would like now to tell you a few instances in the lives of some of these girls who have been uplifted, strengthened and comforted by the Gospel of Jesus Christ.

A little girl was brought to us some years ago; her heathen name had been Issakee, the name of a cruel goddess. Her father had been the priest of a demon shrine, a man of very great influence amongst the people where he lived. But a great change came over the mind of the father. This demon

A very Primitive Travancore Church.

MEMBERS AND CHILDREN OUTSIDE A L.M.S. TRAVANCORE CHURCH.

priest became a thoroughly converted Christian man and an earnest worker. The shrine was pulled down and those fearful idols which they worshipped are now in the Mission House at London, and if ever you are in the Museum there you may see what this heathen girl was taught to worship as a little child. The father became baptized and this little girl and baby brother were baptized too. She was named Anantham, which means "Joy," and when she was twelve years old her father and mother brought her to the Boarding School and left her in the care of the missionary's wife. She learnt for five years until she was nearly eighteen. She reached the head of the school and exerted a sweet influence over her fellow scholars. When she left, the missionary's wife did not like to lose sight of her and she came to the house every week with the embroidery work she had learnt to do so beautifully. Soon after she joined the Church and was the light and joy of the home.

Father and mother were so happy to have this beautiful sweet Christian girl in the home, that they did not wish to part with her, so she lived for two happy years helping her mother and doing her embroidery. She had a class of little children on the verandah of her home, she read her Bible to the ignorant women, she sewed garments for new Christians who had come over through the work of her father and mother, and in every way showed herself to be a bright disciple of Jesus Christ. Do you realize what a difference there had come into that child's life?

CHAPTER VIII

HOW THE CHURCHES GROW

THOSE old pictures that you see sometimes, of a missionary as a white man in a long black coat with an umbrella over his head, standing under a palm tree, with an open Bible in his hand and a crowd of dark-skinned people sitting round him eagerly listening to his words, those pictures are not quite accurate.

In foreign lands they are not more willing to submit themselves to Jesus Christ than many young people are in England. There are thousands of young lives in our land who take all the blessings which come from Christ, without thinking from Whom they come, but they do not give their lives to His service. How then do you think the Gospel is preached in foreign lands? It is by Christian life and example amongst the people.

For instance, near where a certain missionary lived some years ago there lived a poor man who owned a small field. This field lay close to the land of a large landowner and the rich man's lands lay almost surrounding the poor man's little plot. The poor man sowed his field with rice and the rice grew, very much like your corn grows in England, with a long stalk of straw and a rich ear of corn grain, ripening into yellow as the harvest time comes. One of the brightest sights in all the land is a rice field ripening for the harvest. When this poor man's rice was thus growing two bullocks belonging to the rich man, entered the poor man's little plot and ate it up. The poor man, deeply distressed, and in grief, went to the rich man and said, "Sir, your bullocks have eaten up all my crop, my livelihood this season is gone. You must give me some compensation." "Oh, yes," said the rich man, "I'll compensate you." So saying, he turned to two of his servants and said, "Go tie that man to that cocoanut tree!" and they did so. Then he said to another, "Go up that tree and cut some cocoanuts, and put them at that man's feet!" and they did so. Then he said to one of his servants, "Go fetch the village watchman." The watchman came, and the rich man said, "I found this man stealing my cocoanuts and I give him in charge." The servants said they too saw the same, and the poor man was taken to prison.

The missionary, who had not been long in the country, heard of this. He made representations to the Court, he saw that case through, and saw the poor man compensated, and the rich man prevented from doing this great injustice. Now I want you to see the result of that. The poor men all round hearing of this said, "If this man's religion helps him to do things like this, we will go and hear what he speaks about," and so they come one by one and two by two, until they all hear this wonderful story of the great Saviour who came down from the heights of His glory, that He might be the Saviour and Friend of the poorest and most sinful man and woman in the world.

Then some are attracted by words uttered by a way-side preacher, others by some tract they have read, others by coming into contact with earnest prayerful Christians, others who have been sick in our hospitals, and have heard of the Great Physician, and others by the visits of Christian teachers to their village.

A band of preachers went into a village where there was one Christian family, and the villagers said, "We do not need you to teach us about the excellences of your religion, for there is Yesudial living over there and she is living her religion and we know it is good." When men thus get interested they will open their houses for a prayer meeting, where their fellow villagers attend. Then the number of the people becomes a little too large for a house, and a small shed consisting of four posts and a covering of cocoanut leaves is erected. It is called a "four-legged chapel" and the cost is from 5*s.* to 10*s.*, somewhat like the first photograph in this chapter. This is very primitive, but in these places the Gospel is preached with power and souls are converted, and some of my happiest experiences have been in these first beginnings of a Christian church.

As the people grow in numbers and intelligence, these little sheds become too small; there also grows up a feeling in the minds of the people that a place where they meet for prayer should be a little more dignified, and besides they wish for a school in which their children can be taught in the week days. They then begin to raise a fund for the erection of a better place, and the rule adopted is generally, that the people raise two-thirds of the money and the Mission, if it can afford it, will give the remaining third.

For from the beginning they are taught not to expect something for nothing, and in this way attempts are made to develop a spirit of self-reliance. When after a few years they manage to save 90 or 100 rupees and the missionary can give them 50, a small building built of mud, with doors and windows and a roof, well made and covered with thatch, costing altogether about £10, is erected like the second photograph, and we call this a £10 church. This is the usual style of the ordinary village chapel in Travancore, some smaller and some larger, according to the requirements of the people. These are, as a rule, school rooms in the week and churches on the Sunday. They are kept up as schools mainly by the people themselves with a little help from the school funds.

Generally, under the stimulus of some outstanding

NAGERCOIL SCHOOL.

leader among them, the desire arises to have a stone church which shall last for generations and be a witness to the growing power of Christ in the land. This is fostered by the missionary, especially in large and influential centres, and the result is a church, like photograph number 3, which will cost, say, £120 to £150. These larger churches form the central churches of small circles, and it is the earnest desire of all connected with them, that the village churches within a mile or two of these central churches, shall become self-supporting circles. The largest church we have is at Nagercoil, which will hold about 2,500 to 3,000 persons, and one of the sights is to see this church filled at a Communion service on the first Sunday in every year.

These churches have very little furniture in them, except in the most advanced buildings. The members of the church not being used to chairs in their own houses, it has not been thought advisable to adopt a style that would be more expensive than they could afford themselves. In places like Trivandrum, the capital of the state, and Nagercoil, the largest station in our Mission, and in every head church of the different districts, benches have been introduced and they are necessary, but for ordinary churches their use is not encouraged.

The way in which the church at Neyoor was seated was rather amusing. It so happened upon one occasion, that a high-caste man who had received some benefit at the Medical Mission while staying at the hospital, expressed a desire to attend the Sunday service. As there were no chairs, the Missionary had a chair taken in. After the service was over the congregation with very great indignation rose up against the Missionary saying, "that in this way in the very church of God, he

Three of our Lace-workers, Nagercoil.

A Christian Evangelist

An Educated Indian

was giving way to caste feeling, making distinction between man and man, and his action would cause serious trouble."

The Missionary said," This is absurd, because you can all have chairs there if you like." Next Sunday was a sight never to be forgotten. All the members of the congregation came,bringing their chairs behind them, some on three legged stools about four inches high, some on benches two feet high, some on old chairs that they had bought at the bazaars, all sorts and all sizes—benches, chairs, old boxes, high and low, narrow and broad, and the scene inside the church that morning defied description. The service went on and it was pointed out to these people, in the kindest manner, that disorder of this kind could not possibly be permitted, and the result was that a pattern bench was sketched out for them by the missionary and a plan made to provide seats of a uniform size at their own expense. They worked at it with a will and the result ever since has given great satisfaction.

The majority of the Christians in the South come from what are called the " Shanar " class, who occupy a position equal to that of a respectable day-labourer, while some have holdings of land. In the northern part of our Mission, many are from the Pariah and Pulia class.

All of them were demon worshippers, ignorant,

oppressed and degraded. Christianity came to them as a delivering hand, as well as a spiritual message. The missionary was regarded, not only as a centre of spiritual light, but also as a pillar of material helpfulness, and the poor people clung to him as a refuge from oppression, while they listened to his teaching. The result is that we have now in Travancore 368 churches, 76,618 in our Christian community (this includes a self-supporting pastorate, containing 73 congregations and 25,213 people), and the people altogether last year raised 30,000 rupees, or two thousand pounds for the support of God's cause amongst them. So you see from the little church where a solitary Missionary a hundred years ago, .began to preach his Gospel, there has grown this great number of people.

Besides increase of numbers, there is a growth of Christian life and principle, which is very encouraging. For instance—a little time ago, a man came to our house in very great anger against a fellow Christian of his. "This man has deceived me," said he. "In what way?" asked the missionary. "He told me that he would give his daughter in marriage to my son. We had our family meeting about it, and now the man utterly refuses to have anything more to do with us and I have made my preparations." (You must know that in India arrangements for the marriage of the young people are made by the fathers and the mothers.)

"Well," said the missionary, "send for the man." The man came in, walking ten miles to the missionary's house, and he was asked, "Why have you broken your promise?" He replied "Well, sir, it is true I promised to give my daughter to that man's son, but I was anxious to see what sort of a Christian this young man was, and I made it my duty one Sunday to go to his village and attend the church of which he was said to be a member. He was not at the morning service. I made inquiries and found that he was at work in his fields. He came in late to the noon-day service and again he went to his fields. That man, sir, is not a Christian. He does not keep the Sabbath. He is only a nominal Christian. I want a true Christian man for my daughter's husband if I can get one, and I am not going to give her to any man who is not a real out and out Christian man, therefore this engagement is off." The missionary, of course, could not help but sympathize with the man in his desire for his daughter's happiness.

I was summoned once to a high-caste house to see an old man who was very ill, and on my entering the house and speaking to him he said, "Oh, sir! I am so glad you have come. I want you to baptize me." Now I was in a house where the very name of Christ was pollution, and much surprised at this request, I said, "What do you know about Jesus Christ that you should ask for baptism?" His reply was, "Oh, sir, I have been reading about him in the Bible for years, and I am humbly clinging to His feet." I said to his family, "Do you hear what he says? What shall I do?" Their reply was, "Let him do as he likes, sir."

There seemed to be a power in the house holding back all opposition. "Will you bring me a little water and a towel?" They brought it, and I knelt down in prayer, and after prayer I rose and said, "What is your name?" He said "That is a heathen name, sir, I want a Christian name." Still amazed, I began repeating some of the Christian names that we have made, for one of the first things the missionary has to do is to make Christian names in the native language. I repeated some and none seemed to satisfy him until I came to one, Yesudian—that is Yesu-adian. You will see that the first part of this word is Jesus, sweet in every language, but very sweet in Tamil, I think. Adian is a translation of that phrase that Paul often uses, "Paul a servant of Christ." It really means a slave of Christ. "Yesudian" means the humble servant of Jesus.

When I came to that name he said, "Yes, sir, that will do," and there in that house, surrounded

Snake Charmers.

by all his family I baptized that dear old man in the name of Yesudian, the servant of Christ.

You will see that the growth of a church does not mean only increase of church buildings, nor that great numbers are coming under Christian instruction, but it does mean besides that Christian character is being formed. It is true that in this Christian society, the poor have found helpers, the lonely have found a home, and the wretched and despairing have found kindly hearts who loved them for Christ's sake.

CHAPTER IX

LOOKING BACKWARD, AND LOOKING FORWARD

A LITTLE more than a hundred years ago, in April 1806, a lonely man with no earthly possessions but his Bible and his faith in God, was standing upon the borders of Travancore. He was very tired, for he had a long journey of sixty miles from his last station. He had just crossed the frontier and lay down in a rest-house. As he was a white man and a foreigner, he did not know that he was breaking caste rules by seeking rest in this place, but the Magistrate immediately sent word to him to remove, as this was a sacred place to the Brahmins, so he had to move and rest in the open air under the shade of trees.

For three years he worked amongst the poor people, unable to get land to put up a Christian building. He was told that all the country had been given by the King of Travancore to the Brahmins, and that therefore the Magistrate would not give him permission to build a church anywhere in the country. It was only in 1809 that he wrote

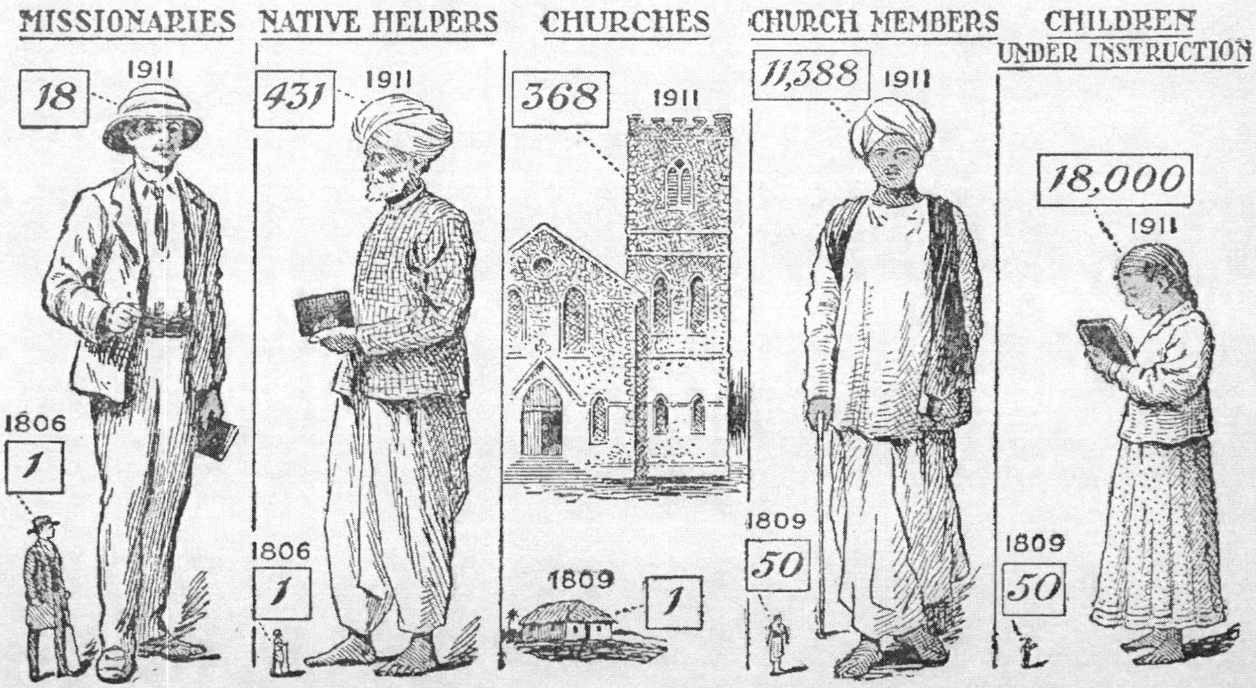
MISSIONARIES
18
1911
1806
1
NATIVE HELPERS
431
1911
1806
1
CHURCHES
368
1911
1809
1
CHURCH MEMBERS
11,388
1911
1809
50
CHILDREN UNDER INSTRUCTION
18,000
1911
1809
50

Bathing in a Sacred Tank.

THE GREAT PAGODA, TRIVANDRUM.

saying, "I have just bought the first land for the first church in Travancore."

Now see the difference. In 1909 a deputation from the London Missionary Society visited Travancore. They came from Quilon, 140 miles from where our first missionary began his work, and all down that 140 miles of country, at intervals of three or four miles, they passed Christian churches connected with our Mission. This is what they say :—

"The Mission was celebrating its Centenary. Everywhere throughout our journey from Quilon to Nagercoil, it was the subject of congratulation and hope. We did not expect such a continuous and constantly repeated expression of joy. In every town in which we stayed, in every village to which we went, it was the chief theme. The climax was reserved for Nagercoil, where the chief meetings were held, and delegates from other Societies were assembled. The Communion Service in connexion with our visit reached the highest point of influence. When the time of the Lord's Supper came, over 1,500 men and women met around the table of the Lord. The meeting was one of the most impressive we have ever known. There was an unmistakable promise of the growing authority of the great kingdom, the victory of light over darkness, of life over death. The seed sown by a Ringeltaube had borne abundant fruit."

Do you not see how great a change has taken place and can you not see how God's promise has become true that " The little one should become a thousand."

In 1910 there was a great meeting of the United Church of South India at Trevandrum, the capital of Travancore, and the representatives of 150,000 Christians sent a letter to His Highness the Maharajah, thanking him for the privilege of meeting in his capital. This is what the Maharajah said to the Christians in reply :

" I have received with pleasure your kind letter on behalf of the General Assembly of the South India United Church, and request that you will be good enough to convey to the President and the members of the Assembly, my cordial acknowledgments of their prayers and their good wishes for the prosperity of my country and myself. It is very gratifying to know your appreciation of the endeavours of my administration to secure the welfare of my Christian subjects.

I am glad that the Assembly meets on this occasion at my Capital, as it testifies to the fact of the spread of the Christian religion in this country. Wishing that the Almighty may crown your labours of love with success,

" I am,

" Yours sincerely,

" RAMA VARMA."

This kindly message from a king, who is devoted to the Hindu religion by birth, conviction and practice, ought to interest the young people of England, because it shows the kindness of his heart and the breadth of his sympathy.

I am sure also we shall all thank God that He has so far blessed the work of His servants. Sometimes you will hear Missionary work sneered at, and if you are trying to be a Christian, even in your own schools, among your own playmates, you may be laughed at, but you must always remember that the greatest influence for good in this world comes from those boys and girls and men and women who have linked themselves to Jesus Christ.

Another thing I want to say is that a new hope was born when our Saviour came into the world, and it is this hope that brightens the lives of all Christian workers. This hopefulness of the Christian is a great perplexity to our Indian friends. A young well educated Brahmin once said to me: "Nothing amazes me more than the hopefulness of the Missionaries. The difficulties in this country in the way of victory are enormous, and yet I have never heard a missionary speak or seen the writings of a missionary without being amazed by the hopefulness with which they speak of winning India to the Gospel." And another man said: "You will never get us Brahmins; look at our priesthoods, look at our temples, look at our vested interests. You may get some of these poor miserable people." My reply was: "I may not get you, sir, but my son will get your son, and I will tell you why—because men are bound by a moral necessity to love the highest when they see it, and Jesus Christ our Saviour is the highest revelation that has come to us from God." Do you not think this is true? If you have ever read Tennyson's "Idylls of the King," you will remember the lament of that sorrowful and guilty queen, whose conduct had worked such terrible ruin in King Arthur's court, and how when she fled away from the king to the Convent at Aylesbury and repented of all she had done, she said, "Oh, God! What might I not have made of Thy fair world if I had only loved Thy highest creature here." We needs must love the highest when we see it, and therefore because our Saviour lived that sinless and supreme life on earth, giving us such radiant ideas of God, such wonderful teachings about man and his destiny, men cannot help following Him when once their eyes are opened to see what He is, what they are and what they may become.

The most educated and the best people amongst the Hindus are realizing that there is something in Christianity that they need. "We must borrow the spirit of love, which comes from Christ." said one. "The Christians," said another, "are strong and powerful because they have one flag, one book, one Saviour, but we have no lodestar on earth and no polestar in heaven." This pathetic confession that they have nothing to attract them on earth, nothing to guide them to heaven is met by those words of our Saviour, "I, if I be lifted up, will draw all men unto me." There is the attractive power of our Saviour. The lodestar on earth drawing out the affection, the love and gratitude of all who wish to live true lives. "In my Father's house are many mansions. I go to prepare a place for you, that where I am there you may be also." This is the polestar in heaven, guiding all Christian souls over the perplexed road of human life into a realm of peace.

Then the hopefulness of the Christian is increased because, as the Bible is being circulated throughout the land, people are more and more reading this Bible, comparing it with their own books, and it is shining by its own light, winning its way into the hearts of the Hindu people. The late Maharajah of Travancore had the reputation of being one of the most learned of all modern Hindu princes. He had great gifts; was a splendid English scholar and a gentleman of sound judgment and great influence. When a young man he used to give lectures to the young men of his country, and in one of these lectures, while he confessed he was not able to accept Christianity as we taught it from the West, yet he said these striking words about the Bible—

"Where do the English people get their knowledge, intelligence, cleverness and power? It is their Bible that gives it to them, and now they bring it to us, translate it into our language and say 'Take it, read it, examine it, and see if it is not good.' They do not force it upon us as the Mohammedans did their Koran, but they bring it saying, 'This is what raised us, take it and raise yourselves.' Of one thing I am convinced, that do with it what we will, oppose it as we may, it is the Christian's Bible that will sooner or later work out the regeneration of our land."

I think it will be seen that while we look back with gratitude on all that has been done, we can look forward with very great encouragement. Our eyes are made for seeing, but a good many people look at things and do not see them at all. We can look on life and upon Christian work with the eye of a slave or with the eye of a prophet. Do you remember that scene on Mount Carmel when the prophet Elijah told his servant to go up the mountain and look out on the far horizon towards the sea. The servant came back and said he saw nothing. "Go up again," said the prophet, and, returning from his seventh journey, he came back at last saying, "I see just a little cloud about the size of a man's hand." That is all the servant, the slave, saw. But the prophet said, "Tell the king to go down quickly," for he saw the heavens black with clouds, the king's chariot stopped by floods of rain and the barren land bright with harvest. The prophet was long sighted, the slave was short-sighted. So you and I may look upon things and not see much meaning in them. It is only as God gives us the longer sight which comes by contact with Jesus Christ that we see the true meaning of our life and work in this world. Many regard the Gospel as the expression of the dying forces of an old superstition, while others regard it as the crowning effort of divine redeeming power.

May our heavenly Father give to the young people of England the sight which our Saviour had of the needs and the possibilities of human life, so that their hands and hearts may be engaged in sweet helpfulness, and may they find it their greatest honour and joy to take up their cross and follow Christ and be fellow-workers with Him in the redemption of the world. Who is on the Lord's side, who will serve the King?

The Communion Service in a Travancore Church.

Ancient Syrian Church at Quilon. Missionary and Syrian Priest.

Watching the "John Williams" coming in at Puka Puka, the loneliest Rarotongan outstation.

THROUGH THE EYES OF THE ISLAND CHILDREN

By BASIL MATHEWS, M.A.

THROUGH THE EYES OF THE ISLAND CHILDREN

BROWN children hop from one foot to another in a perfect wriggle of excitement on the fringing reef of a coral island. Before these brownies the quiet waters of a blue lagoon glitter and gleam in the shining sun. This still lagoon is surrounded by a grim reef of coral on which the great, rolling breakers of the mighty Pacific Ocean crash and boom far away.

The children with the sharpest eyes can see, far beyond the outer reef and across the ocean, a wisp of smoke. Is it a tiny cloud? "No," they cry, "it is 'the Religion Ship,'" as they dance with joy; while some rush back to their thatched cottage homes to call their mothers and brothers out. Soon all the people are running down to the fringing reef shouting to one another—

"It is the *John Williams*!"

Yes, it is the Children's Ship—the best-beloved steamer amongst all the thousand ships upon the oceans of the world. She comes nearer and nearer, then drops a boat into which some of the brown crew quickly jump; and, one after another, passengers are helped down and rowed ashore. Boxes of books follow, with tinned food, biscuits, *News from Afar* and *The Chronicle*, letters from home and clothes for the missionaries. "The pens, the ink and the paper are in the boat," as our French exercise-books say.

Who are these white people round whom the brown children and grown-ups rush, with handshakings and shouts of welcome?

These are two of our missionaries, husband and wife, who have been home in England for rest and change. Now, to the huge delight of their people, the *John Williams* has brought them back again to take up their work in this beautiful island home. They have been obliged to leave their sons and daughters at home in England at Walthamstow Hall and Eltham College. These hot islands are not a good place to make white children grow strong and lively. But the brown children of this Pacific coral island are trying, by their loving welcome, to make up for the absence of the missionaries' own boys and girls.

Look, the people are staggering down to the beach, bearing great loads of strange-looking vegetables. They bring tons and tons of these yams down to the beach.

Are they going to sell them to the crew? No,

they would be quite hurt if we asked them that question.

They have planted, watched, tended and harvested these yams through the year so that they can give them to the *John Williams* for her crew and passengers. They give hundreds of pounds, worth of yams to the ship. Thus they help us children to support the ship. And they do it all without having any New Year Offering gift book promised to them! They do it just for love. Do we?

The yams are on board. The steam whistle of the *John Williams* sounds. The boats are being hurried from the beach. But there are some young South Sea Island men and women now in the boat, in addition to the crew! On the beach older men are waving their hands, and old women are softly crying.

The young brown men and women who have gone off in the boat to the *John Williams* are leaving home themselves to go as missionaries to the far-off, wild, cannibal, savage Papuans. Their old mothers are weeping on the beach because they know that many and many a young couple who have gone—as their sons and daughters are going—to teach the children and grown-ups of Papua, have never returned. For the evil fevers have killed them. Then is it worth while for them to go at all?

Let us sail with them on the *John Williams* and see. We visit island after island in the Pacific, and everywhere we see the children laugh and clap their hands when they see the ship that they love.

What different kinds of islands these are that we see! Here is one where we can steam along fairly close to the fringing reef of the island itself, though we must not get too near, for it was on just such a reef as this that the first *John Williams* was ground to pieces by the waves.

But here again is quite another kind of island, like that which we described first of all, for it has a great circular barrier reef, and then a shallow lagoon all the way round the island, and then inside that a fringing reef, with its cocoanut palms on it, and rising up into a mountain behind a great rocky piece of land uplifted many, many years ago by some long-dead volcano.

A third kind of island, which we will call a lagoon island or atoll, is different again, for this one is just a great broken fringing reef with a broad lagoon in between, but no central Island.

Off one of the Samoan Islands we see a swift little motor-boat, and in it, dressed in his rough sea-going overalls, the Rev. J. W. Sibree and his little boy Gordon. This motor-boat, the *Tuasivi*, you can see in the big full-page picture.

THE L.M.S. FLEET IN THE SOUTH SEAS.

At last we turn the screw of the *John Williams* to the islands and her bow towards Papua, the British part of the enormous island off the north of Australia, where New Guinea looks like a great clumsy turtle on the map.

While we are ploughing through the sea westward from the islands to Papua we shall get a good chance of pestering Captain Steele with questions. There he is, coming down from the bridge. Now then.

"Captain Steele, would you please tell us how many feet long the *John Williams* is. How old is she, how fast does she go, and why does she have sails as well as engines and a funnel, and please——"

"Steady, steady," says Captain Steele, who is not only a good ship's captain, but can set a broken leg, conduct a service, make a speech, give you medicine to make you better, and do quite a number of other things.

"Not more than six at a time, please," he says with a smile. "The *John Williams* is 185 feet long.

"She was built and launched in 1894, and went round England to the principal seaports before coming out to the Pacific, so that the children of England could see their ship. She can travel nine knots an hour, but usually we do not drive her more than eight. She has sails, so that when we have a good favourable wind we can use them and save up the coal so that the London Missionary Society shall have as little expense as possible. But we are bound to have steam, because sometimes the wind is against us and sometimes it is calm when we want to hurry on.

"It was just because they had not got steam engines that the first *John Williams* was carried by the current on to the coral reef and wrecked, for the sea is so deep outside the reefs that it is impossible to use an anchor."

"Thank you, Captain Steele, and what are those funny wires stretched across from the masts?" He explains to us that this is the wireless telegraphy apparatus which is now fitted to the *John Williams*, What Captain Steele does not tell us is that he himself gave the apparatus to the ship, and for this we must all thank him very much.

Now we have been sailing and steaming for nine days, and are nearing the shores of Papua. We come to Kwato, where the Rev. C.W. Abel works and where the first of the brood of little speedy motor-boats comes out to meet us. We shall meet a number more along the coast of Papua as we travel in the *John Williams*. You will see most of them in the full-page pictures, and you can find their names in the key of that picture.

This one is the *Mamari*, which is a local word of friendly greeting. *Mamari* being painted on the bow of the boat is just as though the boat were ready to rub noses (or bows) with everybody and say: "How are you?" "I hope you are very well!"

There are some native Papuan boys in this boat, and they are very proud to-day because they have made and launched two new life-boats which you will see placed on the deck of the *John Williams* for her use. One of these boats they have given themselves, and the other has been paid for by the Young Men's Missionary Hundred in Sydney.

Mr. Abel's boat is not in the picture, but it is the same size as the *Ainauia*, which will meet us at the next station.

We come next to Fife Bay, where the Rev. C. F. Rich has his fine new motor-boat, the *Ainauia*, to help him to carry the story of Jesus to the multitudes of people along the hundred miles of broken coast-line on which he works. Mr. Rich used to have to travel in an open whale-boat, which was very unhealthy in this particularly wet and hot piece of country.

The word *Ainauia* means "The Gift." This is because it was a "gift" from people in England for Mr. Rich's work under the London Missionary Society, and because it goes to take the gift of the Gospel of peace and love to the people of Papua.

The *Ainauia* belongs to the navy of peace, and it was very thrilling when she was launched at Portsmouth to see her pass under the stern of Nelson's old warship, the wooden *Victory*, and across the path of the *Indomitable*, a Dreadnought battleship.

As we pass along by Kerepunu, Vatorata, Port Moresby and Delena and Ukea, we find at each station boats, mostly whale-boats, rowed by boys, which carry the missionary along the coast to do his work. When we reach Orokolo, where Mr. Bartlett lives, we see him come out in his swift boat the *Malara*, and as we approach we hear a sound which we never expected to hear in this far-off land, the sound of the Orokolo Pioneer Band: the boys playing a tune on their fifes. These fifes are a present to Orokolo from the London 60th Company Boys' Brigade, and now the Pioneer Band of New Guinea, which practises twice a week, plays the whole village to church every Sunday with its twenty fifes, four native drums and a home-made triangle. It is playing because the boys are so glad to see the *John Williams*.

Waving "good-bye" to Mr. Bartlett, we come to Urika Island, where the Rev. J. H. Holmes goes among the people of the river on board his *Purari*

TYPES OF ISLANDS (Sections)

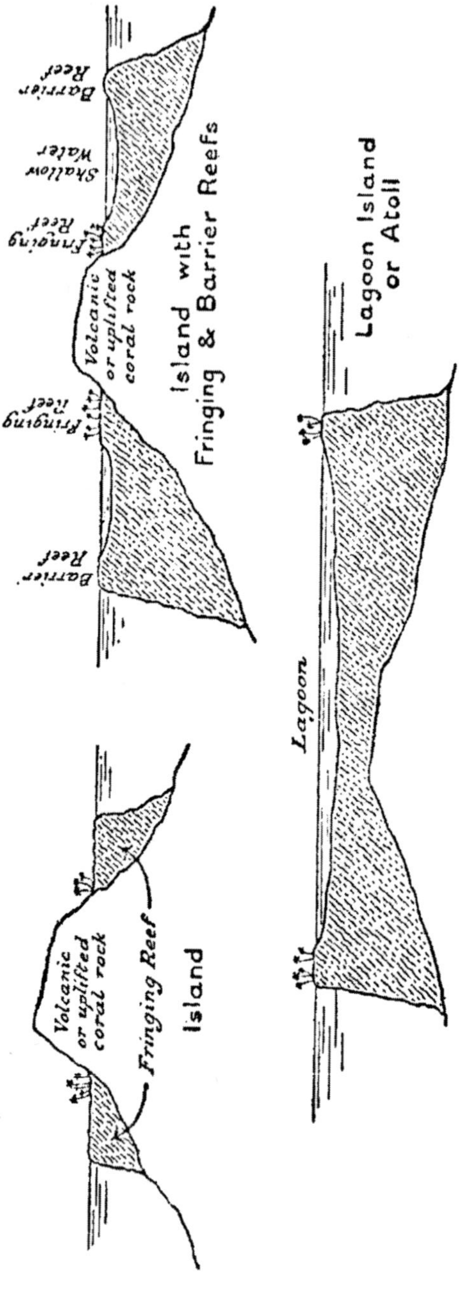

launch. *Purari* is the name of the river at the mouth of which is Urika, the L.M.S. island.

Many a cannibal of that wild country, when he steps on board the *Purari* to come to Urika, steps for the first time out of awful heathenism into the pure atmosphere of our Christian village, where the youths learn to forsake their old work of breaking each other's heads for the really much more enjoyable task of making furniture, boats and houses.

The thickly-populated country just round here is to be opened up by still another motor-boat which is called the *Tamate.* This, as you know, is the native name of the great hero James Chalmers, who was killed by the cannibals. Mr. Butcher, up to this last year, has used a small sailing cutter named the *Pearl,* with a speed of about four miles per hour. Now he has for the first time this fine, roomy, seaworthy motor-boat, the *Tamate,* 48 ft. long by 10 ft. wide, with a depth of 6 ft., with two cabins, including a wardrobe and cupboards, steward's pantry, and with a speed of nine knots per hour.

This will be much more healthy for Mr. Butcher in the fever-stricken river-streams, and will help him to visit twice as many people.

You will have seen that at most of the stations we have passed there are South Sea Island pastors and teachers living as missionaries to the Papuans. But they have not only given pastors and teachers and also yams for food for the crew and passengers. For the people of Niuè, the island in the South Seas which Captain Cook called Savage Island, have collected money to build a fine sailing vessel, which you see in the accompanying picture. She is called the *Niuè*, and has done wonderful work in the past sailing up and down this wild broken coast and carrying the missionaries from place to place. Without her many and many a boy and girl who is to-day living a joyful, useful life at one of our missionary villages would be still grovelling in the darkness and swamps of cannibal Papua.

It is for the support of the *John Williams* and these other boats that we boys and girls in Britain every year collect our New Year Offerings, and this book which is in your hands is the gift book of the London Missionary Society sent out to those who collect, in recognition of their work.

I hope that you have read and enjoyed this book and its delightful pictures. I hope, too, that even if it was for the sake of getting this book that you began collecting for the ships, you will, when you collect next year, gather in the money not because you are going to get the book, but simply for love; because you want to carry out to those who live on the far-off islands of the South Seas and in the steaming swamps of Papua the light and the joy and the happiness that come to you through the companionship of our Hero and Friend and Saviour Jesus Christ. Let us keep the Flag of Peace—the Flag of the Three Doves—fluttering in the breeze on the mast of the *John Williams*. Now, Captain Steele, full steam ahead, for the boys and girls of Britain are at work to support the Fleet.

Printed by BUTLER & TANNER, *Frome and London.*